PRAISE FOR

TENSION CITY

"[A] brisk and engaging memoir . . . *Tension City* provides a vivid peek at behind-the-curtain clashes."

—*The Washington Post*

"A candidate's every phrase and physical movement is dissected by campaign officials, political strategists, journalists and others. . . . Who better to provide a thoughtful and revealing examination of these uniquely American electoral exercises than Jim Lehrer, a man who has moderated a whopping 11 of them?"

—Associated Press

"Lehrer describes this intersection of politics, performance, and journalism with plenty of delicious behind-the-scenes details."

—*Publishers Weekly*

"In his quiet but intense way, Jim earns the trust of the major political players of our time. He explains and exposes their hopes and dreams, their strengths and failures as they tried to put their best foot forward."

—BARBARA WALTERS, *ABC News*

"Unique and compelling. Jim Lehrer at once enlightens and entertains, deepening our understanding of the modern presidency while telling a splendid story. *Tension City* is engaging history from a fair-minded and insightful author who has himself become part of the nation's fabric."

—JON MEACHAM,
author of *American Lion*

"Wit and perspective that only a natural born storyteller can summon. Some of the most interesting presidential debates take place off-camera, around the reporters asking the questions. For instance, Lehrer goes behind Bernie Shaw's jaw-dropping inquiry directed to Michael Dukakis about the hypothetical rape and murder of the candidate's wife. That's just one of the revelations that makes this the ultimate insider's account of what George H. W. Bush dubbed 'tension city.' It's all here—Gerald Ford's premature liberation of Poland, Ronald Reagan's way with one-liners, the well-honed empathy of Bill Clinton."

—RICHARD NORTON SMITH,
author of *The Colonel*

"Jim Lehrer is a national monument, and this riveting book shows how he became America's moderator. *Tension City* is at once Lehrer's behind-the-blue-curtain account of his central role in almost a dozen presidential debates and an original, brisk inner history of recent American politics, combined with important lessons on how to moderate anything—all told in Lehrer's famously wry and authoritative voice. Each page of Lehrer's book benefits from his unparalleled experience as a key player, and his extraordinary ability to view these fabled confrontations with the detachment, insight, humor, and ironic sense of a wonderful writer."

—MICHAEL BESCHLOSS,
author of *Presidential Courage*

TENSION
CITY

TENSION
CITY

★

INSIDE
THE PRESIDENTIAL
DEBATES

Jim Lehrer

RANDOM HOUSE TRADE PAPERBACKS | NEW YORK

Published in the United States by Random House Trade Paperbacks,
an imprint of The Random House Publishing Group,
a division of Random House, Inc., New York.

RANDOM HOUSE TRADE PAPERBACKS and colophon are
trademarks of Random House, Inc.

Originally published in hardcover in the United States by Random House,
an imprint of The Random House Publishing Group,
a division of Random House, Inc., in 2011.

LIBRARY OF CONGRESS CATALOGING-IN-PUBLICATION DATA

Lehrer, James.
Tension city: Inside the presidential debates / Jim Lehrer.
p. cm.
Includes index.
ISBN 978-0-8129-8143-8
eBook ISBN 978-0-679-60351-1
1. Campaign debates—United States. 2. Presidents—United States—Election.
3. Television in politics—United States. 4. Lehrer, James. I. Title.
JK524.L44 2011   324.7'3—dc22   2010015080

Printed in the United States of America

Title-page images: copyright © iStockphoto.com / © liangpv (top),
copyright iStockphoto.com / © Nicholas Monu (bottom)

www.atrandom.com

2 4 6 8 9 7 5 3 1

Book design by Victoria Wong

To Kate, and Jamie,
Lucy, and Amanda

"Those big-time things . . . it was tension city, Jim."

—former president George H. W. Bush
in an April 10, 1999, interview

Contents

Introduction

"Good evening from the Magness Arena at the University of Denver in Denver, Colorado. I'm _____ of _____ and I welcome you to the first of the 2012 presidential debates between President Barack Obama, the Democratic nominee, and former Massachusetts governor Mitt Romney, the Republican nominee. . . ."

Thus, on October 3, a moderator will begin the nationally televised candidate debates of the important 2012 presidential election. There would be three more "Good evenings" before the month was over—two presidential at Hofstra University in Hempstead, New York, and Lynn University in Boca Raton, Florida, plus the vice-presidential debate at Centre College, Danville, Kentucky.

But whatever happens during those four evenings, I believe this year has already been a breakthrough one for presidential debates.

Campaigns for presidential nominations used to be shoe-leather operations. The only voters touched directly in the past were mostly those eligible to vote in Iowa, New Hampshire, and South Carolina.

No more. They have now been nationalized.

I believe the loud, unkempt televised debates among the candidates for the 2012 Republican nomination are mostly responsible. Like it or not, those twenty events between May 2011 and February 2012 turned out to be the most pivotal happenings of the GOP race.

No, they were not always pretty. There was a quality of *The Good, the Bad and the Ugly* to them. Several resembled high-rent game show television. All but one of the events were distractingly raucous. Some treated individual candidates unfairly.

Yet front-runners came and went because of what happened during the debates. Fiery momentum was ignited behind some candidates but extinguished forever for others. Issues of substance and character, as well as simple intelligence, wit, and likability were exposed on a see-for-yourself comparative basis.

That exposure was enormous—and paramount. Most of the individual debates had national television audiences of more than five million, several more than six million, and one even reaching as many as seven million viewers. Those are substantial numbers in any political league, but particularly that of primary politics television. Republicans and independents watched to make choices, Democrats to sneer and jeer, and everyone else to simply be informed—or, in some cases, to be entertained.

Whatever their reasons, the millions had much to watch, including, in the last four debates, Newt Gingrich, Ron Paul, Mitt Romney, and Rick Santorum, who became doubly known as the GOP version of college basketball's Final Four.

There is no question in my mind that these twenty debates yielded a substantial residue worth sifting through for important lessons.

First, there is little question that the general atmosphere was often negative. Some people came to the debate hall to cheer, hiss, and boo, and they even seemed encouraged to do so. This often resulted in candidates reaching for an applause/cheer line rather than the substance point, which in turn trod all over the purpose of the debate, namely the exchange of ideas and positions as opposed to a contest for whose supporters could make the most noise.

The sponsoring broadcast news organizations also spent too much time with opening music and gaudy graphics. Did the producers need to be reminded that the public did not need to be sold on watching what they were already watching?

And because the co-sponsors were mostly political party and partisan interest groups, much of the valuable questioning time was also wasted on long/multiple introductions, acknowledgments, thank-yous, and various public displays.

Not all moderators were equally effective. Some simply talked too much. Others tried too hard to prove how tough they were. Brian Williams of NBC, at a debate in Tampa, was the only moderator to keep the hall audience silent.

Most important, I think the majority of the pre–Final Four events were unfair to all but the front-runner candidates. The center positions onstage, the lead-off questions, and most of the airtime went to the candidates who were leading in the polls on that particular evening, a practice that began with the 2008 Democratic primary debates. There were twenty-six in the year between April 2007 and April 2008, and Barack Obama and Hillary Clinton were permitted to suck up most of the airtime from John Edwards, Joe Biden, Chris Dodd, and Bill Richardson, as well as Dennis Kucinich and Mike Gravel.

I believe all debates should be conducted as if among equals. The whole point of the presidential primary debates is to weed the candidate field by allowing potential voters to see *all* of the candidates in action and interaction. Straws should be drawn for the candidate positions onstage. Announce at the beginning that the moderator(s) are determined to keep the airtime among the candidates as equal as possible. And hold to that promise.

Also, I strongly recommend that it be standard practice to advise debate hall audiences in advance that they are expected to remain absolutely silent during a debate. They are invited guests, not participants. The moderator should remind the would-be cheerleaders and boobirds of the rules and enforce them when necessary. That has been the long-established practice in the fall general election debates.

The place of presidential nomination debates in the world of important consequences really did begin with those Democratic debates of 2008. Barack Obama was not the best debater of the first event in Orangeburg, South Carolina, on April 26, 2007. Clinton, Dodd, Biden, Edwards, and even Kucinich were clearly better than the junior senator from Illinois. But he *got* better with each debate afterward, and that was a major reason he was one of only two candidates present for the last debate on April 16, 2008, in Philadelphia. The other, as we know, was Hillary Clinton.

The pundits and the pros have had a major go at speculating

on how President Obama's 2012 reelection chances have been helped by the twenty Republican debates. No sifting of the residue can ignore the potential impact the candidate attacks on one another could have on the general election outcome in November.

But serious minds and wannabe candidates must resist the temptation to use that 2012 line as an argument for curtailing the number of either party's primary debates in 2016. I believe that for nomination pickers of all persuasions, the more debates, the better. Think neutrally. Unexpected strengths as well as serious weaknesses were discovered in the course of those twenty 2012 Republican debates. Without multiple debates, important character and issue differences might never have seen the much-needed light of day—or night.

That point goes right along with why all presidential nomination debates should be viewed—and produced—as events that substantially impact the election of the president of the United States, the most important exercise of our American democracy.

They are not game shows. They really do matter.

Meanwhile, on to Denver—and to the many more "Good evenings" beyond.

Jim Lehrer
Washington
June 2012

TENSION
CITY

CHAPTER 1

Good Evenings

"Good evening. The television and radio stations of the United States and their affiliated stations are proud to provide facilities for a discussion of issues in the current political campaign by the two major candidates for the presidency. The candidates need no introduction. The Republican candidate, Vice President Richard M. Nixon, and the Democratic candidate, Senator John F. Kennedy."

That was how the moderator, Howard K. Smith of CBS, opened the first televised presidential debate from the studios of WBBM-TV, Chicago, on September 26, 1960.

"Good evening from the Ford Center for the Performing Arts at the University of Mississippi in Oxford. I'm Jim Lehrer of *The NewsHour* on PBS, and I welcome you to the first of the 2008 presidential debates between the Republican nominee, Senator John McCain of Arizona, and the Democratic nominee, Senator Barack Obama of Illinois."

That was how I began the first McCain-Obama debate on September 26, 2008—nearly fifty years later.

There have been thirty-five nationally televised presidential and vice presidential debates, counting that first in 1960 and the last four in 2008.

All the moderators have been broadcast journalists except one—*Chicago Sun-Times* editor James Hoge in 1976. There have been several repeaters: Howard K. Smith of CBS and ABC, Edwin Newman of NBC, Barbara Walters of ABC, Bernard Shaw of CNN, Bob Schieffer of CBS, my PBS colleague Gwen Ifill, and I account for twenty-one of the thirty-five moderating assignments.

Our "Good evenings" have remained roughly the same—except for the top billing going to the geography.

"Good evening from the Wait Chapel at Wake Forest University in Winston-Salem, North Carolina."

"Good evening from the Bushnell Theater in Hartford, Connecticut."

"Good evening from the University of Miami Convocation Center in Coral Gables, Florida."

The first of my greetings was for a 1988 debate between Vice President George H. W. Bush and Governor Michael Dukakis in Winston-Salem.

That was when I got my introduction to the terrors and triumphs of moderating presidential debates, an experience I have sometimes compared to walking down the blade of a knife.

At Winston-Salem, it actually started before the debate itself.

I was closeted behind a closely guarded conference room door with my three debate colleagues—Peter Jennings of ABC, Annie Groer of the *Orlando Sentinel,* and John Mashek of *The Atlanta Constitution*—to discuss our questions for Bush and Dukakis. This was before the coming of the single-moderator format; the standard arrangement was a moderator plus panelists.

Jennings, anchor of ABC's *World News Tonight,* had an act of provocation on his mind.

He urged the four of us to forget the rules that had been agreed upon between the candidates and the Commission on Presidential Debates. We should publicly—in front of the whole world—invite Bush and Dukakis to take on each other directly with no time limits on questions, answers, or anything else.

I said we couldn't do that. We had given our word to follow the rules of the debate. Not to do so, I insisted in my most righteous tone, would be dishonorable, among other things.

Annie Groer and John Mashek agreed. Jennings quickly went along, with grace and professionalism.

Also in Winston-Salem, my wife, Kate, helped with some much needed pre-debate personal perspective that remains with me to this day.

In the hotel, as we were leaving for the debate, I came down with a bad case of nerves. I whined to Kate about how terrible the pressure was on me.

She said, quite calmly, "If it's bad for you, think what it must be like for those two candidates—one bad move and they lose the presidency of the United States."

True.

But I was still left with the pre-debate anxieties that have been with me in every one of the ten presidential and vice presidential debates I have moderated since. I soon learned that dealing with nerves is *the* key to being able to function effectively as a moderator. My guess is that there are surgeons, classroom teachers, and short-order cooks among the huge crowds of other people who know exactly what I'm talking about. Possibilities of pleasure and satisfaction, horror and failure, await everyone who performs.

The incredibly high stakes are what magnify it all in presidential debates. Candidates and their attendants have only one overriding purpose—to win the election to be the most powerful person in the world. But others, including most in the serious press and political science worlds, see debates as decisive opportunities to inform and educate the voters about whom to grant such power.

The critical space between those two very different purposes is the battleground on which all combat occurs.

"UGLY, I DON'T like 'em."

That's how George H. W. Bush categorizes his debate experience.

"Why not?"

"Well, partially I wasn't too good at 'em. Secondly, there's some of it's contrived. Show business. You prompt to get the answers ahead of time. Now this guy, you got Bernie Shaw on the panel and here's what he's probably gonna ask you. You got Leslie Stahl over here and she's known to go for this and that, I want to be sure I remember what Leslie's going to ask and get this answer. . . . There's a certain artificiality to it, lack of spontaneity to it. And, I don't know, I just felt uncomfortable about it."

That exchange was one of the many I have had with the candidates after their presidential and vice presidential debates. The interviews, done over a period of twenty years, began as an oral history project with the Commission on Presidential Debates. Portions were later used in *Debating Our Destiny,* a two-hour PBS documentary that was first broadcast in 2000.

George W. Bush's view differed from his father's.

"I think it's useful for people [to] watch and see how a person they don't know stands up and answers questions and deals with the thrusts and parries of the debate. I actually also think you can learn what the person really believes. I think they are very useful."

Ronald Reagan was also positive. "The people have a right to know all they can in comparison to make a decision," he said. "If the debate is concentrated on the major issues and the views of the two individuals on those issues, then it is of service to the people."

Bill Clinton and Bob Dole, in their separate interviews, said debates help make for better candidates.

"I think they force us to prepare," said Dole. "They force us to think about issues we maybe hadn't focused on—they force us to think ahead."

Clinton went even further: "Even if these debates don't change many votes and, you know, normally both sides do well enough so they can avoid any lasting damage, but having to do them and knowing that if you blow it, they will change a lot of votes, forces people who wish to be president to do things that they should do. And I am convinced that the debates I went through, especially those three in 1992, actually helped me to be a better president."

George H. W. Bush, after further thought, favorably compared debates to competitive athletics, which he said he always loved. There was an adrenaline flow during debates similar to that triggered by sports—particularly tennis.

Jimmy Carter also offered a sports comparison: "I think I did go in as though it was an athletic competition, or a very highly charged competitive arrangement."

So did Gerald Ford, who said, "I had that experience many times playing football for the University of Michigan, and that was my attitude before that first debate. I felt comfortable with the positions I would take, and I was anxious to get into the ball game."

Al Gore, Ross Perot, and Lloyd Bentsen were the only candidates missing from our postmortem debate interviews.

Bentsen, the 1988 Democratic nominee for vice president, very much wanted to talk to us but was by then too ill from a stroke to do so. With former vice president Gore, we tried every ploy we could think of and went through every channel we could find, but he declined to discuss his several debate experiences as a vice presidential and presidential candidate. So did Ross Perot, who as an independent made it to the presidential debates against President George H. W. Bush and Governor Bill Clinton in 1992.

In addition to Bob Dole and former presidents Reagan, Ford, Carter, Clinton, and both Bushes, I also questioned former vice presidents Mondale, Quayle, and Cheney, plus John Kerry, John Anderson, Geraldine Ferraro, Jack Kemp, Joe Lieberman, John Edwards, and James Stockdale.

Most of the conversations concentrated on Major Moments,

as they've come to be called—happenings during specific debates that drew the most attention and seemed destined to find their way into political histories.

Presidential debates are the ultimate Rashomon exercises, of course. Each participant remembers a debate performance through the prism, emotional as well as political, of his or her own place at the podium—or table, chair, camera, or microphone.

That goes for those who ask the questions as well as those who answer them.

The first ever nationally televised debate moderator, Howard K. Smith, spoke mostly as an observer/reporter when recalling his 1960 Kennedy-Nixon debate experience. In a 1996 memoir, *Events Leading Up to My Death,* he wrote, "Having the two appear live, side by side, answering the same questions, was a welcome innovation. But it was not much of a debate. Because the reporters on the panel were not allowed to pose follow-up questions, both candidates shamelessly slid by questions rather than answering them."

Smith said it was obvious from the moment the two entered the Chicago studio that Nixon realized he should never have agreed to the confrontation. He was the incumbent vice president and much better known than Kennedy. Appearing together would only elevate Kennedy's status.

Also, Nixon had been in the hospital and was pale, Smith said. "I offered a makeup expert, but he refused and allowed an aide merely to dust a little powder on his face, which made him paler. He was downcast; he knew it was a mistake."

Kennedy, meanwhile, "entered the studio looking like a

young athlete come to receive his wreath of laurel." Addison's disease had added a tan tint to his skin, and the steroids he took for back pain had caused him to fill out.

Smith said of Kennedy, "He later told me he won the election that night."

That is also the conventional wisdom among many political historians, keyed to the fact it had more to do with looks than words. Neither Kennedy nor Nixon opened up any major differences over policy that dominated their campaign before or during the debate. Politically, both were running—and mostly seen—as no-boat-rattling centrists.

More than one hundred million Americans followed the debate, and those who listened to it on the radio thought Nixon had won.

Nixon didn't go so far as to say that the perception of the first debate cost him the election, but he hinted at it. He wrote of the 1960 campaign in his 1962 memoir, *Six Crises:*

"I paid too much attention to what I was going to say and too little to how I would look."

Those are words to live by that a few post-1960 candidates have ignored at their peril.

THE NEGOTIATED AGREEMENT for the four Kennedy-Nixon events set future patterns for formats and almost everything else about the debates until 1992—including the negotiations themselves.

As a matter of history, even Abraham Lincoln and Stephen

A. Douglas tangled over the specifics of the subject, the number, and some of the details of their seven famous Illinois debates on slavery in 1858. They did their pre-debate negotiating through the mail and surrogates—not that much differently than the way it still happens.

In 1960, surrogates for Nixon and Kennedy wrestled with the debate sponsors—the commercial television networks—over the room temperature, the use of notes, and the lighting, among other things. The biggest hurdles were over the number of debates and the selection of the journalist moderators and panelists. Kennedy wanted more debates than Nixon; the networks wanted only TV/radio questioners, while the candidates insisted on bringing print people into the mix, as well.

Kennedy and Nixon stood behind podiums, made opening and closing statements, and, in between, answered questions that were solely the work of the individual panelists. No questions or specific topics were cleared ahead of time with anyone—most particularly the candidates.

Debate formats differed little through the years between 1960 and 1992, the major variables confined to answer time limits and the addition of a live audience. The four Kennedy-Nixon exchanges were all in silent television studios.

In 1988, moderators were allowed to move beyond traffic-cop and follow-up duties to ask their own opening questions of each candidate. I was the first moderator to do so.

The October 15, 1992, debate among President George H. W. Bush, Bill Clinton, and Ross Perot changed everything. For the first time, candidates would answer questions created and asked by would-be voters, not professional journalists, in a town hall–type format. Carole Simpson of ABC News moderated that event at the University of Richmond, Virginia.

The opening half of the October 19, 1992, ninety-minute Bush-Clinton-Perot event at East Lansing, Michigan, which I moderated, was the first presidential debate with no major time restraints—no two-minute answers and one-minute responses. That followed a week after the raucous vice presidential debate among Dan Quayle, Al Gore, and James Stockdale, which featured a five-minute discussion period about each issue. Hal Bruno of ABC moderated that one.

Those debates also marked the end of the journalist-panel format. Simpson, Bruno, and I all sat alone at the moderator's table at our respective events. Every debate since—in 1996, 2000, 2004, and 2008—has had either a sole moderator or a participatory "town hall" audience.

The only other new wrinkle has been to have the candidates do at least one of their debates seated at a table rather than standing at podiums. During the George W. Bush years, all vice presidential debates were seated, a pattern that began at the insistence of Dick Cheney, as the Republican candidate for vice president in 2000 and again as the incumbent four years later.

While the 1992 wide-open "experiment"—a podium debate—appeared to work at the time, it has yet to return in any future debate. According to those involved in negotiations since, most candidates, each in their own way, choose not to take what is considered "the risk" of an open format.

There were no presidential debates for sixteen years after the Kennedy-Nixon four. Their return almost immediately proved that some risks cannot be negotiated away.

THERE STOOD JIMMY Carter and Gerald Ford at their podiums on September 23, 1976, at the Walnut Theater in Philadelphia.

And the audio failed.

Carter and Ford remained standing onstage for twenty-seven minutes without exchanging a word or much more than an occasional glance the whole time.

I asked both men—in separate 1989 interviews—what that had been like.

"I watched that tape afterward," Carter remembered, "and it was embarrassing to me that both President Ford and I stood there almost like robots. We didn't move around, we didn't walk over and shake hands with each other. We just stood there."

Said Ford, "I suspect both of us would have liked to sit down and relax while the technicians were fixing the [sound] system, but I think both of us were hesitant to make any gesture that might look like we weren't physically or mentally able to handle a problem like this."

Carter added, "So I don't know who was more ill at ease, me or President Ford."

I said it looked like a tie to me.

"It *was* a tie," Carter agreed. "Neither one of us was at ease, there's no doubt about that. Those events, I think, to some degree let the American public size up the candidates, and I don't think either one of us made any points on that deal."

Edwin Newman of NBC News moderated that debate. He said afterward that he had never been in such a tricky situation. He did, in fact, ask Carter and Ford if they wanted to sit down in chairs on the stage while they waited for the sound to return.

"Not only did they not sit down, they did not acknowledge that I had suggested it," Newman said.

CARTER AND FORD each went on to produce his very own Major Moment in the two following debates that 1976 fall. Both were about substance—not style.

Ford's was clearly the *more* major of the two. It was in the second debate in San Francisco. One of the press panelists, Max Frankel of *The New York Times,* asked Ford about the recently signed Helsinki agreement that seemed to acknowledge "the Russians have dominance in Eastern Europe."

Ford answered that the thirty-five-nation pact did not mean any such thing.

"It just isn't true. . . . There is no Soviet domination of Eastern Europe and there never will be under a Ford administration."

Frankel questioned if he really did hear Ford say that Eastern Europe was not under Russia's sphere of influence.

Ford replied, "I don't believe, Mr. Frankel, that the Yugoslavians consider themselves dominated by the Soviet Union. I

don't believe that the Romanians consider themselves dominated by the Soviet Union. I don't believe that the Poles consider
themselves dominated by the Soviet Union."

The press and most everyone else in the world of politics
clobbered Ford.

Later he tried to clarify what he meant: "There is no question I did not adequately explain what I was thinking. I felt very
strongly that regardless of the number of Soviet armored
divisions in Poland, the Russians would never dominate the Pol-
ish spirit. That's what I should have said. I simply left out the
fact that at that time in 1976, the Russians had about ten to fifteen divisions in Poland."

Did Carter realize there on the stage that night what President Ford had done?

"Yes, I did. And I was prepared to jump in, you know, and
take advantage of it. But just on the spur of the moment, I realized that it would serve me better to let the news reporters question President Ford's analysis and judgment."

I asked Ford, "Did you have any idea that you had said
something wrong?"

"Not at the time. Not at the time. In retrospect, obviously,
the inclusion of a sentence or maybe a phrase would have made
all the difference in the world."

Carter recognized it was a serious mistake, but did the election turn on it?

"I don't know if it did or not, because there are so many fac-
tors that can enter a campaign, but certainly it cost him some
votes, and, as you know, the election was quite close."

"We ended up losing by only a point and a half, or maybe two points," Ford added. "So any one of a number of problems in the campaign could have made the difference."

Carter's own Major Moment occurred during the third 1976 debate in Williamsburg, Virginia.

Playboy magazine had just published an interview in which Carter said, "I've looked on a lot of women with lust. I've committed adultery in my heart many times. This is something that God recognizes I will do—and I have done it—and God forgives me for it."

Carter, in his interview with me, said he knew that could cost him the election. He realized—as he said in the debate itself when asked by Robert Maynard of *The Washington Post*—that it was a mistake to have given the interview in the first place.

"I thought the best way to handle it was to say, well, I'm sorry that the interview came out, but I couldn't deny that the answers in *Playboy* were my own answers."

The consensus was that, in the end, Carter's admission pretty much blunted the damage from the *Playboy* interview.

Barbara Walters moderated that third 1976 Carter-Ford debate at Williamsburg.

In her 2008 memoir, *Audition,* she put that debate into a fascinating personal workplace context.

She recounted how she was living a nightmare then as the first woman nightly news anchor. Her ABC coanchor was Harry Reasoner, whose hostility toward Walters had become a public story and was obvious to anyone who even glanced at the screen when they appeared together.

"I don't know whether the League [of Women Voters] chose me out of pity or because they thought I would do a good job, but, boy, did I need that vote of confidence," she wrote. "The debate went smoothly. I did not make a flub or a misstep. I slept soundly that night for the first time in a long time and flew back to New York refreshed and ready for new battles."

Whatever else, the debates of 1976 were important just because they happened.

They began the move toward the political imperative that there must be presidential debates. The sixteen-year debate hiatus was mostly the result of front-runner incumbents Lyndon Johnson and Richard Nixon deciding they only had something to lose by sharing a stage with Barry Goldwater, the Republican nominee against Johnson in 1964, or Hubert Humphrey, the Democratic challenger to Nixon in 1968.

Ford, in 1976, was an incumbent, having been the appointed vice president who become president upon Nixon's resignation. But because of the Watergate scandal and Ford's pardon of Nixon, incumbency was no asset for Ford. He was the one who challenged Carter to debate.

"I had to do something to overcome the thirty-some points I was behind," Ford said in our interview.

Carter said he was reluctant to accept. "It was a very disturbing concept for me to be onstage with the president of the United States. I've never even met a *Democratic* president in my life, so there was an aura about the presidency that was quite overwhelming."

MEANWHILE, THE RUNNING mates of Ford and Carter made their own history in 1976 by becoming the first vice presidential candidates to debate on national television.

Walter Mondale, the Democrat, and Bob Dole, the Republican, faced each other on the stage of the Alley Theater in Houston. There were Major Moments—mostly Dole's.

The Kansas senator joked that while he was chairman of the Republican Party during Watergate, the event happened on his night off. He also used humor to take an indirect hit on Carter for the *Playboy* interview:

"I couldn't quite understand what Governor Carter meant in *Playboy* magazine. I couldn't understand frankly why he was in *Playboy* magazine. But he was and we'll give him the bunny vote."

The largest Dole Moment, however, was no joke. He proclaimed Vietnam, Korea, World War II, and World War I were "all Democrat wars" that resulted in 1.6 million killed and wounded, "enough to fill the city of Detroit."

Mondale said that he had actually anticipated such a charge from Dole. "Unbelievable. I had to try to keep a straight face. I think they blew the election right there. One of my advisers—I'll never forget this—we were just closing down the last [predebate] discussion, and he said, 'I'll bet that Senator Dole will accuse the Democrats of causing World War II,' and I said, 'You are crazy.' He said, 'No, I've got a feeling he'll do it.' So I said, 'Well, how shall we handle it?' "

He handled it that night by saying Dole had just showed why his reputation for being a hatchet man was richly earned and that the American people clearly did not believe there was a partisan difference "over involvement in the war to fight Nazi Germany."

I asked Dole how he happened to say "Democrat wars."

"It was boilerplate," Dole replied. "I mean, in those days, you know, I had a stack of briefing notes about two feet high, which . . . I received from the Ford people, the national committee, and I guess I should have exercised my own judgment. But, in any event, I probably wish I hadn't said it."

"You *do* wish you hadn't said it?"

"Yeah. One of my heroes was FDR and I'm a World War II veteran, so I didn't want . . . to run around and say, well, the Democrats started all the wars in the world."

Dole acknowledged that he was known as Ford's hatchet man and maybe he deserved such a label. "But Ford had sort of the Rose Garden strategy and I was out in the briar patch. I used to tell him, you know, please call me home."

Because of the "Democrat wars" exchange, Mondale left the Houston stage certain that the Carter-Mondale ticket had won the election right then and there. It was over.

Dole didn't feel that strongly about it. He did review a tape of the Houston debate but concluded that he really didn't go over the line. "But I must say it made me more cautious in future debates."

That vice presidential debate charted some new ground for the questioners. Hal Bruno, then of *Newsweek,* Walter Mears of the Associated Press, and Marilyn Berger, then of NBC News, were the panelists. James Hoge, the editor of the *Chicago Sun-Times,* was the moderator.

Bruno said they met the day before the debate to compose

questions, but they did not know in advance what order they would each be asking.

"So we put them on index cards, and when we got to the hall we dished them out once we knew the order," Bruno said. "I ended up asking the first question, but Walter had written it. It worked pretty good—the debate followed a logical sequence."

That set a pattern of cooperation on questions among debate panelists that held—mostly—from then on.

JIMMY CARTER WAS the incumbent in 1980, and he was faced with two challengers who wanted to debate him—Republican Ronald Reagan and John Anderson, a moderate Republican congressman from Illinois running as an independent.

Carter was willing to debate Reagan but not Anderson.

As he explained to me, "President Reagan only wanted one debate, and he wanted it as late as possible. And whenever we pursued the subject of a debate, he said, well, we can't have a two-person debate since John Anderson is running as an independent. We've got to have him on as an equal candidate. And obviously, Reagan knew that every time the independent candidate got a vote, it was a vote taken away from me."

As a result, on September 21, 1980, only Reagan and Anderson stood on the debate stage in Baltimore.

I asked Reagan why he went ahead with the Anderson debate. "They wanted a three-way debate, and Carter refused to do that one, and I didn't see any reason why Anderson should be excommunicated," he said. "So I said no, I would go forward with it. It became just a two-way debate."

Anderson maintained later that he understood what Reagan was up to. "Well, I think that he felt that perhaps it made him look as the person to be admired for being forthright and open and willing to take on all comers. And in contrast to that, Carter was being very defensive, felt beleaguered, and was unwilling to expose himself to a three-person debate."

Reagan conceded that Carter, the man who wasn't there, had to endure unanswered criticism from both him and Anderson at the Baltimore debate—particularly about the failing economy. "There might be some feeling of unfairness about this, because he was not here to respond. But I believe it would have been much more unfair to have had John Anderson denied the right to participate in this debate."

Meanwhile, Carter's campaign people insisted on one-on-one debates with Reagan.

"I wanted a lot of debates," Carter said. "I wanted three or four debates at least."

Why?

"Because I thought that I was much more a master of the subject matter. I knew that he was a master of the medium, perfectly at ease before the television cameras. I knew that I was not a master of the medium, and I thought that if we'd get past the one hour and go to maybe four, five, six hours on television, that substance rather than style would be more prevalent."

In the end, there was just one Carter-Reagan debate at Public Music Hall in Cleveland one week before Election Day. The moderator was the same Howard K. Smith who had moderated the first Kennedy-Nixon event in 1960. The only thing that had changed in twenty years was the network. Smith had moved from CBS to ABC.

Smith, in his memoir, said, "The actor had it all the way," adding, "That night Reagan won the debate and, as they say, put the election on ice."

John Anderson was struck immediately with the certainty that the Reagan-Carter debate had devastated his campaign. "The only thing that I could think of was that on the television sets as people across the country watched that debate, it was a two-man race. If I had been important, if I had really been other than simply tangential to the whole process, I would have been there. They didn't know about all of the back-and-forth and the efforts that we had made to get into the debate. They couldn't possibly know the disappointment that that was. No, it was absolutely crushing."

Two Major Moments came from that one debate.

Carter's came when he said, "I had a discussion with my daughter, Amy, the other day, before I came here, to ask her what the most important issue was. She said she thought nuclear weaponry—and the control of nuclear arms."

That was a blunder that Carter himself later acknowledged.

"It was an honest statement that made a point that still is remembered. I got a flood of letters afterward, you know, congratulations, you did the right thing. Your daughter, Amy, had more judgment about nuclear weaponry than Reagan did and so forth. But I think in the contest there just a few days before the election, he came out ahead on that deal."

Reagan knew it the moment Carter said it.

"It seemed to me he had [made a terrible mistake], because the whole thing sounded—and I think you could almost feel an attitude from the audience on it—that the president was going to make a major policy based on what a child told him. And I'm sure he didn't have that in mind, but that's the way it came out. And I was prepared to say to the people, I promise them I wouldn't ask my kids what I should do."

That was also the night of Reagan's most famous debate line, "There you go again."

The subject at that moment was a proposal concerning Medicare and Carter's repeated charge that Reagan had opposed even its original creation on the grounds that it was socialized medicine.

CARTER: Governor Reagan again, typically, is against such a proposal.

MODERATOR SMITH: Governor?

REAGAN: There you go again. When I opposed Medicare, there was another piece of legislation meeting the same problem before the Congress. I happened to favor the other piece of legislation and thought that it would be better for the senior citizens and provide better care than the one that was finally passed.

But for the two men, in their separate interviews with me, there was no agreement on that telling line.

"Well, I'm sure that was a well-rehearsed line that President

Reagan had prepared carefully," Carter said, citing "the style of delivery when he would bring it in . . . it was an inevitable statement that he would make."

Reagan denied he had prepared to use those specific words in advance. "No, it just seemed to be the thing to say in [response to] what he was saying up there, because . . . to me it felt kind of repetitious, something we had heard before."

Carter conceded the damage. "That was a memorable line. I think it showed that he was relaxed and had a sense of humor, and it was kind of a denigrating thing for me. And I think that he benefited from saying that, politically speaking."

Reagan's view was that his own closing point in that debate—suggesting that voters ask themselves whether they were better off now than they were four years ago—was more important to his winning the debate, and, ultimately, the election.

FOUR YEARS LATER, Walter Mondale, as the 1984 Democratic nominee, had the daunting task of facing Republican president Ronald Reagan, who maintained a strong lead in the polls.

Barbara Walters, moderator of the first Reagan-Mondale debate, highlighted another difficult task—getting the candidates to agree on the journalist panels.

After laying out the format and the rules, she said to the vast television audience, "And now I would like to add a personal note, if I may. As Dorothy Ridings [president of the League of Women Voters] said [in her introduction], I have been involved now in four presidential debates, either as a moderator or as a panelist. In the past, there was no problem in selecting panelists. Tonight, however, there were to have been four panelists participating in this debate. The candidates were given a list of almost one hundred qualified journalists from all the media and could agree on only these three fine journalists. As moderator, and on behalf of my fellow journalists, I very much regret, as does the League of Women Voters, that this situation has occurred."

For Mondale, the stakes were high. He figured his only hope was that something would happen during the debates to turn things around. He also knew Reagan, the front-runner incumbent, didn't have to debate him at all. The debate imperative was not yet that established.

BUT REAGAN AGREED to two debates in October, in the last few weeks before the election. One was in Louisville, Kentucky; the other in Kansas City, Kansas.

Mondale went into those debates with a hard, fast mission.

"I wanted to show presidential stature," he told me. "I wanted to show mastery of the issues. I wanted to show that progressive dimension again. I wanted to show that I was more alert than the president, without being negative."

The former vice president was also ready for Reagan's signature line. In the first debate in Louisville, Mondale suggested that Reagan would propose a tax increase on low- and middle-income Americans after the election, leaving wealthy Americans largely untouched.

REAGAN: You know, I wasn't going to say this at all, but I can't help it: There you go again. I don't have a plan to tax or increase taxes. I am not going to increase taxes. I can understand why you are, Mr. Mondale, because as a senator you voted sixteen times to increase taxes. . . .

Reagan continued along these lines, and panelist Fred Barnes of *The Baltimore Sun* pressed him for details on his commitment not to raise taxes in his second term. Mondale, during his rebuttal, pounced.

MONDALE: Mr. President, you said, "There you go again." All right. Remember the last time you said that? You said it when President Carter said you were going to cut Medicare, and you said, "Oh no, there you go again, Mr. President." And what did you do right after the election? You went out and tried to cut $20 billion out of Medicare. And so, when you say "There you go again," people remember this.

Mondale happily agreed with the debate consensus that he had won the debate. But he said there was more to it than his prepared comeback. "The main thing, I think, that hurt him was he seemed to be ill-focused, seemed to lose his way, stumble, roam around in irrelevancies, and it was a pretty—it was an impressively unimpressive personal performance."

Others had noted that Reagan seemed tired. I asked him about that.

"No, it wasn't tired. I was overtrained. . . . I want to tell you, I just had more facts and figures poured at me for weeks before than anyone could possibly sort out and use, and I call it overtraining. When I got there, I realized that I was racking my brain so much for facts and figures on whatever subject we were talking about that I knew I didn't do well."

But two weeks later in Kansas City, things changed. Reagan said later he definitely did not go into that one overtrained. And panelist Henry Trewhitt of *The Baltimore Sun* asked a question that enabled him to turn a potential liability into a strength:

> TREWHITT: You already are the oldest president in history, and some of your staff say you were tired after your most recent encounter with Mr. Mondale. I recall yet that President Kennedy had to go for days on end with very little sleep during the Cuba missile crisis. Is there any doubt in your mind that you would be able to function in such circumstances?
>
> REAGAN: Not at all. And, Mr. Trewhitt, I want you to know that also I will not make age an issue of this campaign. I am not going to exploit, for political purposes, my opponent's youth and inexperience.

When I asked if he had been lying for that one, Reagan said it just came to him right off the top of his head.

Whether the line was preprogrammed on not, Mondale knew he had just taken a hit.

"Well, I'll tell you, if TV can tell the truth, as you say it can, you'll see that I was smiling. But I think if you come in close, you'll see some tears coming down because I knew he had gotten me there. . . . That was really the end of my campaign that night, I think. That's what I thought."

That night?

"Yes, I walked off and I was almost certain the campaign was over, and it was."

Did you say that to anybody?

"My wife."

MY INTERVIEW WITH Ronald Reagan took place five years after the 1984 debates in his Century Plaza office in Los Angeles. There was already talk that the former president was having memory problems and, in fact, one of his own aides suggested to me not to expect a full accounting of every little thing that had happened in every debate.

Reagan implied that himself as we chatted before the cameras started taping. It was clear that somebody had to force him to talk about the debates in the first place. Let's just get it over and be done with it, his body language suggested.

Making small talk, Reagan mentioned that he had just autographed—for the makeup artist—an old copy of *Photoplay* magazine that featured him and Paul Muni on the cover. Reagan amused everyone by recounting how Muni had always insisted on standing on the left-hand side for all group studio stills, as it offered a "better angle."

I brought up that just a month before, by chance, I had watched his 1940 movie *Santa Fe Trail* on television.

Reagan gave me one of those famous smiles and recounted

with considerable detail how he had posed for a *Santa Fe Trail* group cast photo that included Errol Flynn, Raymond Massey, Olivia de Havilland, Alan Hale, and Van Heflin. Reagan played Custer; Flynn was Jeb Stuart.

He told me that Errol Flynn, "as always," had insisted on posing in the front row in the most prominent position. Both were tall, but Reagan, behind Flynn, wanted to appear to tower over him. So he stood on a small box of some kind. Reagan held up his hands to show the size of the box and raised his head as he had to appear even taller.

He continued talking like that for several delightful minutes, and I think we both had private regrets that we had to move on from his movie memories to presidential debates.

CHAPTER 2

Killer Question

George H. W. Bush, the man who hated debates, had his first against Geraldine Ferraro in 1984.

Ferraro had her own reasons for not looking forward to their vice presidential debate. When considering the possibility of being nominated, "I said the only thing that would scare me in a campaign or running the country is that debate that you'd have to do during the campaign," she said in our post-debate interview.

She was a New York Democratic congresswoman making history as the first woman on either major party's presidential ticket, and she felt it.

"The responsibility that I had at that point, Jim, was I think rather unique. It was more than the fact that I was the vice presidential candidate on a ticket that was challenging the incumbent person, the vice president, but here I was as the first woman and, you know, I was standing in for millions of women in this country. If I messed up, I was messing it up for them."

Bush was also mindful of the enormousness of what was happening on that October 11, 1984, evening at the Civic Center in Philadelphia. He later claimed that of all his six debates, that one was the most tense.

Why? I asked.

"Well, I think the press was automatically divided. I think a lot of the females in the press corps said this was one of us. You could hear them clapping [in the] room behind."

"Press people were, press people were applauding?" I responded in disbelief.

"Absolutely, the spinmeisters were behind the scene listening as the journalists were clapping and it was . . . a tough one."

Ferraro went into the debate concerned about her knowledge of world affairs. In fact, that was what eventually led to a Major Moment in the debate. Bush had criticized Carter's handling of the Iran crisis and Ferraro knocked Reagan's response to the marine barracks bombing in Beirut.

BUSH: Let me help you with the difference, Mrs. Ferraro, between Iran and the embassy in Lebanon. In Iran, we were held by a foreign government. In Lebanon you had a wanton, terrorist action where the government opposed it. . . .

MODERATOR SANDER VANOCUR: Congresswoman Ferraro.

FERRARO: Let me just say, first of all, that I almost resent, Vice President Bush, your patronizing attitude that you have to teach me about foreign policy.

Was "patronizing" part of a rehearsed line? Bush thought so: "Don't patronize, don't patronize me. . . . I think she was ready. She'd probably been rehearsed for that, and I can't even remember what it was. . . . I said let me help you with that or something. And all that brought the crowd to its feet."

Ferraro denied it was rehearsed. "Absolutely not. No. I was forced into it. I was forced into it because . . . he was trying to teach me about foreign policy but I was knowledgeable, and I didn't need a man who was vice president of the United States and my opponent turning around and putting me down."

I MODERATED BUSH'S next debate, against Michael Dukakis for president in 1988, with the Jennings-Groer-Mashek panelist team in Winston-Salem.

"Those big-time things . . . it was tension city, Jim," was the way he described his entire debate experience.

The moderating moment I most remember from Winston-Salem was my really lousy opening question:

"Our questions this evening will be about equally divided between foreign and domestic policy matters. The first question by agreement between the two candidates goes to Vice President Bush. It is a domestic question. You have two minutes to answer, sir. The polls say the number one domestic issue to a majority of voters is drugs. What is there about these times that drives or draws so many Americans to use drugs?"

It was pure wonk—a perfect start for a think-tank panel discussion but hardly a terrific way to open a presidential debate. The sounds I heard of groans and of television sets switching off all over America were probably not just imagined.

My dismay was compounded by the fact that I was the first

moderator ever allowed, by the negotiated rules, to ask a question on his or her own.

Mashek of *The Atlanta Constitution* soon showed up my question for what it was—puny. He asked Bush, "Mr. Vice President, the Democrats and even some Republicans are still expressing reservations about the qualifications and credentials of Senator Dan Quayle of Indiana, your chosen running mate, to be a heartbeat away from the presidency. What do you see in him that others do not?"

Now it was the sounds of "Ouch!" being heard throughout the hall—and the land.

BUSH: I see a young man that was elected to the Senate twice, to the House of Representatives twice. I see a man who is young, and I am putting my confidence in a whole generation of people that are in their thirties and forties. . . . So judge the man on his record, not on a lot of rumors and innuendo and trying to fool around with his name. My opponent says J. Danforth Quayle. Do you know who J. Danforth was? He was a man that gave his life in World War II. So ridiculing a person's name is a little beneath this process, and he'll do very well when we get into the debate.

DUKAKIS: Well, when it comes to ridicule, George, you win a gold medal. I think we can agree on that.

BUSH: Just the facts.

DUKAKIS: But did I—did I sense a desire that maybe Lloyd Bentsen ought to be your running mate when you said there are three people on your ticket?

BUSH: No, I think the debate ought to be between you and Lloyd.

DUKAKIS: I think the American people have a right to judge us on this question—on how we picked our running mate, a person who is a heartbeat away from the presidency. I picked Lloyd Bentsen, distinguished, strong, mature, a leader in the Senate, somebody whose qualifications nobody has questioned. Mr. Bush picked Dan Quayle. I doubt very much that Dan Quayle was the best qualified person for that job. And as a matter of fact, I think for most people, the notion of President Quayle is a very, very troubling notion tonight.

Hits had been coming thick and fast since Bush announced Quayle as his running mate. Everything from the Indiana senator's grades in college and his limited National Guard service as well as his political experience and qualifications to be vice president had been raised—and raised again.

There was another bad moment for me during that Winston-Salem debate.

Bush was answering a Peter Jennings question about the Reagan-Bush record on foreign policy when I interrupted to say his time for answering was up.

BUSH: I still have a couple of minutes left. And there's a difference principle—

LEHRER: Sorry, Mr. Vice President.

BUSH: It's only on yellow here. Wait a minute.

The vice president was right. I had misread—mis-*seen,* to be more accurate—the time cue. There were small colored lights on the cameras for the candidates and a matching set on my desk in front of me. They always started green, then a timekeeper switched them to yellow when a few seconds remained and red when the time was up.

I apologized and told Bush to continue. But he had lost his train of thought—thanks to me.

"I'm finished!"

Bush was understandably annoyed.

But all of that was small potatoes compared to what happened at the second Bush-Dukakis debate at UCLA's Pauley Pavilion eighteen days later.

POLITICAL WRITERS JACK Germond and Jules Witcover gave it a name that stuck—"the killer question"—in their book *Whose Broad Stripes and Bright Stars?: The Trivial Pursuit of the Presidency, 1988.*

Moderator Bernard Shaw of CNN was the second moderator ever permitted to ask an original question. He began: "The first question goes to Governor Dukakis. You have two minutes to respond. Governor, if Kitty Dukakis were raped and murdered, would you favor an irrevocable death penalty for the killer?"

There is now a universal recollection that everyone who was watching had a breath hitch or some kind of "Oh my God!" reaction.

And they reacted again—in disbelief or surprise—as they heard Dukakis calmly, without even a hint of emotion, answer:

"No, I don't, Bernard, and I think you know that I've opposed the death penalty during all of my life. I don't see any evidence that it's a deterrent, and I think there are better and more effective ways to deal with violent crime. We've done so in my own state, and it's one of the reasons why we have had the biggest drop in crime of any industrial state in America, why we have the lowest murder rate of any industrial state in America."

Kitty Dukakis complained to reporters afterward that the question was outrageous, but her husband continued to view it as fair.

"Oh sure," he told me later. "Sure. I mean anybody like me, who is opposed to the death penalty . . . should be subject to that kind of a question. I think it is a perfectly legitimate question."

Why did he answer the way he did?

"Well, if you have been against the death penalty as I have, and this has been an issue in virtually every campaign I've ever run in, you are asked that question, or a variation of it, about a thousand times. And I had been. Unfortunately, I answered it as if I'd been asked it a thousand times."

You answered it as an issue question?

"Yeah."

Bush saw it the way most viewers did. "Mike Dukakis seemed flustered by it, and instead of saying I'd kill him if I could get my hands on him, there was some kind of politically correct answer. And I think that hurt him."

Did Dukakis wish he had handled it differently? "Yeah, I

guess so. On the other hand, I've listened and watched myself respond to that, but I have to tell you—and maybe I'm just still missing it or something. I didn't think it was that bad. You know. But maybe it was. And again, I think you have to be aware of the fact when you are debating, and you have, say, a couple of debates, that a huge number of people are watching you and although you've been answering these kinds of questions all during the campaign, or for that matter all during your political career, for many people, it is the first time they have had a chance to look at you. And so, I think you have to be sensitive to that. And obviously, I wasn't."

I also asked Shaw about his question. Did he have any second thoughts now about that Kitty Dukakis question—twenty-one years later?

Shaw answered immediately: "I don't have *first* thoughts about it. I spent two days working on that question. I tried to mesh the question's thrust with some key issues of the campaign—capital punishment, crime, law and order."

I reminded Shaw that Kitty Dukakis had said right afterward that it was an outrageous and inappropriate question. Others had criticized it, too. He took that in stride.

"When you moderate a presidential debate, you become the center of a bull's-eye. Criticism is expected because of the partisanship involved in the vying for the White House. It didn't surprise me. It didn't bother me. I was concerned that a lot of people didn't take time to look at the thrust of the question."

And then he recounted what happened ten years later—in 1998—when he was coanchoring a political debate for CNN at the Dorothy Chandler Pavilion in Los Angeles.

Shaw said he didn't know it at the time, but Kitty Dukakis was in the audience. After the debate, a CNN executive brought her over.

"He introduced us as if we didn't know each other," Shaw continued. "And while we were there talking—on her own—she said, 'You know . . . that question you asked ten years ago was a fair question. Mike didn't handle it well.' That was away from the angst of the battle."

From there I stumbled across an interesting backstory involving Shaw and the three panelists—Ann Compton of ABC, Andrea Mitchell of NBC, and Margaret Warner, then of *Newsweek,* now a *PBS NewsHour* colleague of mine.

I asked him about reports that the three panelists had tried to talk him out of asking the Kitty Dukakis question as he had written it.

Shaw said that was true. It happened in a pre-debate session aimed at making sure his and the panelists' questions didn't overlap.

"I've never confronted any of the three panelists. But I was outraged at the time that a journalist would try to talk a fellow journalist out of asking a question. I think you can tell I am still doing a burn over it. I just wouldn't think of doing that."

I could indeed tell from the rising force in Shaw's voice that the burn remained.

"They had their reasons. I think as women they were concerned about the question. They did, collectively, ask if I could drop her name. 'Do you have to mention her name?' And, of course, mentioning her name was essential to the whole question."

Compton, Mitchell, and Warner said to me in separate 2009 interviews that while some memories of the exact details had faded with time, Shaw's story was essentially correct.

Compton recited what she called her "Kodak moments" from that 1988 experience.

One was when she, Margaret Warner, and Andrea Mitchell first heard Shaw read them *the* question. It was in Compton's room at the Westwood Marquis Hotel near UCLA where they had gathered to compare notes on questions each might ask. At first, she said Shaw had declined to come to the meeting on the grounds that "we are all professional journalists and we do not need to write each other's questions."

Shaw said to them that he decided to attend just to listen, but as the discussion went along he revealed that his Dukakis question was on the death penalty and his one for Bush was on taxes.

Compton said, "We go on talking and, finally, he says, 'Well, let me tell you my question. And he says, 'If Kitty Dukakis was raped and murdered . . .' I remember the reaction. We all went ahhh! Margaret said 'That gave me chills.' It was the use of the name 'Kitty' that made it . . . such a dramatic question."

"I was stunned—and I recoiled," Warner said to me twenty-one years later. "I have thought about it since then as to why. I think it had to do with being a woman and what it would be like to hear your name said with that kind of question asked about you while sitting there."

Mitchell recalled, "It was the women against Bernie. The use of the words 'rape' and 'murder' . . . it all came together and affected the women differently than it did the one man."

Compton said she and the two others were clearly concerned, but he wouldn't talk about it any further.

After the meeting they went to the debate site, Pauley Pavilion, for a technical walk-through. "As we came into the greenroom afterward, Andrea came back at the question again. 'Bernie, would you at least consider taking her name out of the question, making it less personal—someone you knew?' And he was adamant. 'No.' "

Compton had one more conversation with Shaw about the Dukakis question while they were standing downstairs at their hotel waiting for the cars to drive them to the debate.

" 'I'm sorry you don't like my question,' he said. I said to him: 'Bernie, it's a showstopper. I think it will just seize the debate right at the beginning.' "

That may very well be what Shaw had in mind, she said later. He had left no doubt that he was unhappy about the debate rules that allowed him to ask only one question of each candidate and then become a traffic cop.

"I had the impression that he thought he should be part of a rotation and ask every fourth question. He did not say let's change it [the rules], but he was clearly chafing when we first got there."

The plea to change his question was not the only issue still burning with Shaw years later. The other came up when I asked about his reluctance to share his questions with the three panelists.

"My concern was that this would get back to the candidates," Shaw said. "I suggested that we take a vow that what we discuss in this room does not get out of this room—we do not discuss with editors, producers, or anybody. Everybody agreed. But that was not the case."

On a flight from Los Angeles to Washington the morning after the Dukakis-Bush debate, he sat next to Hal Bruno, who had been a panelist in the 1976 vice presidential debate when he was with *Newsweek*. Now he was ABC's political director and, as such, a colleague of Ann Compton's.

"Hal tells me that he knew the question I was going to ask Dukakis. When my ears heard those words my stomach just tightened. My stomach did a double fist. He indicated they had discussed it within their political unit."

Shaw said he seethed throughout the flight and has continued to do so ever since, but he had never raised his suspicions with anyone before now—including with Compton. He said he had remained cordial with her when they saw each other socially in Washington. "I know why I have never asked her about it is because I get angry every time I think about it," he said.

He thought often about what would have happened if his question had leaked to the Dukakis campaign and how that might have affected the presidential debate.

"From that came a seminal lesson. I will never again, no matter what the circumstances, never again will I ever show anybody, anybody a question I am going to ask in a debate if I'm the moderator," Shaw said.

Ann Compton just as forcefully denied that she had leaked the question to ABC News or anyone else.

"I can guarantee you, I did not utter a word to anyone—not to my husband, to anyone outside the other panelists and Bernie." She acknowledged that it was understandable that

Shaw might have incorrectly "put the two ABCs together" and jumped to the wrong conclusion. "I can guarantee you I breathed not a syllable, nor would I. It would have been the worst breach of ethics."

But Hal Bruno, now retired from ABC, told me that Ann Compton had, in fact, talked to him about the Kitty Dukakis question ahead of time—on the afternoon of the debate.

He had gone to Pauley Pavilion in his official ABC News capacity to, among other things, offer his colleague any assistance she might need.

"Ann and Andrea were distraught—really upset. They were all three upset. They told me that Bernie was going to ask, 'If Kitty Dukakis was raped and killed would you then favor the death penalty?' I said, 'Jeez, that's a terrible question'— something like that. They asked if I could talk him out of it. I said, 'No, I can't. I wouldn't even try.' It just wasn't the right thing to do. It would be improper. When I was a panelist I didn't want anybody telling me what I could or couldn't ask."

Margaret Warner insisted she has no recollection of talking to Hal Bruno or anyone else about Shaw's question ahead of time. "I am shocked that anyone leaked it. I didn't tell anyone— not Hal Bruno nor anyone else."

Mitchell said the same thing. "I definitely don't recall any conversation with Hal Bruno. That would have been odd. He worked for a competing network."

And we are left with the sticky she said/he said situation of differing recollections from five of the nation's top journalism professionals.

The take-away lesson, as I see it, is simply that we journalists are no different from the people we interview. We, too, can see, hear, and interpret differently the same exact events. We, too, have Rashomon-like memories that are not always clear—or precise.

Whatever Shaw's fears, there is not a shred of evidence that anyone from the Dukakis campaign knew the Kitty Dukakis question was coming. The best confirmation, perhaps, is Dukakis's answer. Had he known, would he really have given such a bland and deadening response?

Hal said, "I did not hear anything that indicated *anybody* else knew in advance—no, not at all."

"I know for a fact that it didn't get to the Dukakis campaign," Mitchell said, "because they were quite taken aback by it."

Warner and Compton agreed.

Some final postscripts from my 2009 conversations add to the killer question saga. Bruno and Shaw both grew up in Chicago and have a long professional friendship. Each respected the other as a journalist.

"On that plane the next morning Bernie kept justifying the Dukakis question," Bruno said. "Finally, I said, 'Bernie, that was a shitty question.'" Bruno believed Shaw stuck with the question for its shock value. "He wanted to toss a hand grenade—and he did. He could have done the same thing [asked about capital punishment] in so many different ways with other wording."

Shaw later recounted an exchange he had with Margaret Warner a year after the debate. They were both in a press security line in Warsaw, Poland, while covering a 1989 trip by President George H. W. Bush.

"Margaret Warner, to her credit, walked up to me and she said, 'You know, I've been thinking about that question . . . and I think it was a fair question.' And I said, 'I really appreciate that.' "

Warner confirmed the substance of the Poland chat but did not recall using the specific word "fair":

"I had heard through the grapevine that Bernie was really upset at being challenged by us—and he had taken it personally. I particularly wanted him to know that I had real respect for him as a journalist and that, on balance in retrospect, it was the right question to ask. He had elicited with that question exactly what people go to a debate to find out."

A second "Kodak moment" occurred for Ann Compton as Shaw was cued to start the debate.

"I was sitting right next to him. I didn't know whether to look up. It would be hard to look at Dukakis. So I looked at my hands—at my notes—not knowing where the camera would be. I really thought right up until that last moment that he will modify the question. But he read it exactly as he had told it that morning. . . .

"We heard this gasp behind us from the audience."

Bruno was also looking at his hands.

"Kitty Dukakis was sitting right smack in the front row—in front of the press platforms, where I was," he said. "I knew that question was coming. I had to look away. I didn't want to watch her face. And he asked it. I turned around and looked, of course, and . . . aw, man, she was just anguished so."

Warner's recollection of sitting on that debate stage centered on Dukakis's answer, not Shaw's question. "It was as if he had just turned into a block of ice," she said.

Mitchell described Dukakis's response as "bloodless—flat."

Did the killer question and answer affect the election result?

"I leave that to other interpreters," Bernard Shaw answered when asked.

But *Washington Post* political writer David Broder weighed in with certainty the morning after the debate, according to Ann Compton.

"Ann, the election's over," Broder said. "Dukakis's answer—the election's over."

Hal Bruno went even further: Dukakis's entire performance that night was at fault.

"He had his last chance, and going into that debate we all knew it was going to be his last chance. The way he came across that night—I felt he had not solved his problem. He was somebody who just wasn't in touch and had no connection to where people were. He had blown his last chance."

Germond and Witcover, the creators of the "killer question" term, wrote that Shaw's question—unintentionally—gave Dukakis a chance to neutralize the successful Bush campaign charge that the former Massachusetts governor was "a soft-headed, coldhearted bureaucrat who would be more protective of criminals than of their victims."

Their conclusion: "But because Dukakis failed to take advantage of the dramatic question, a consensus developed almost at once that the second debate, and that first question and answer particularly, had sealed his fate."

Former president Bush was kinder.

"I shouldn't be critical of him, 'cause I'm sure I make plenty of mistakes. But I think that particular answer stands out as one—at least in my memory—that might have been a so-called defining moment. I don't know whether it changed any polling numbers or anything like that."

Dukakis himself deserves the last word here.

"We all screw up at some time in a campaign. And you know, what really defeated me, in my judgment, was just the fact that I didn't take those [soft-on-crime] attacks seriously. I wasn't ready for them. I didn't have a clear sense of how to deal with them, and I think if I had done so, that question would not have defeated me."

THE OCTOBER 5, 1988, vice presidential debate between Republican Dan Quayle and Democratic senator Lloyd Bentsen at the Omaha Civic Auditorium produced still another Major Moment that lives on from that election.

Judy Woodruff, both then and now my PBS colleague, moderated the debate. Like Shaw and me before her, she got to ask each candidate one question. She opened with Quayle.

"Senator, you have been criticized, as we all know, for your decision to stay out of the Vietnam War, for your poor academic record. But more troubling to some are some of the comments that have been made by people in your own party. Just last week former secretary of state [Alexander] Haig said that your pick was the dumbest call George Bush could have made. Your leader in the Senate, Bob Dole, said that a better qualified person could have been chosen. Other Republicans have been far more critical in private. Why do you think that you have not made a more substantial impression on some of these people who have been able to observe you up close?"

Next, it was Bentsen's turn.

"What bothers people is not so much your qualifications but your split on policy with Governor Dukakis. He has said that he does not want a clone of himself, but you disagree with him on some major issues: aid to the Nicaraguan Contras, the death penalty, gun control, among others. If you had to step into the presidency, whose agenda would you pursue, yours or his?"

Woodruff realized, in retrospect, that both of her questions were clearly too long. She said she had tried to cram too much into each—particularly the one to Quayle—in order to back up what she was asking.

"That was a mistake," she said.

She also caught heat from Republicans, who charged that her question for Quayle was much rougher than Bentsen's. She does not accept that.

"I asked the candidates about what I thought were the two major challenges for each. Quayle's was his experience; Bentsen's was his policy differences with Dukakis."

Woodruff's press-panel colleagues followed up her Quayle question—and followed up and followed up—about his readiness, should he have to eventually assume the presidency.

Finally, Quayle reacted.

"Three times that I have had this question and I'll try to answer it again for you as clearly as I can. . . . It is not just age, it's accomplishments, it's experience. I have far more experience than many others that sought the office of vice president of this country. I have as much experience in the Congress as Jack Kennedy did when he sought the presidency. I will be prepared to deal with the people in the Bush administration if that unfortunate event would ever occur."

Bentsen saw a perfect opportunity.

"Senator, I served with Jack Kennedy. I knew Jack Kennedy. Jack Kennedy was a friend of mine. Senator, you're no Jack Kennedy."

And there it was—one of the most quoted debate statements in political history.

As the audience—at least the Democrats there—applauded, Quayle said, "That was really uncalled for, Senator."

That drew Republican applause.

But Bentsen didn't back off.

"You're the one that was making the comparison, Senator. And I'm one who knew him well. And frankly I think you're so far apart in the objectives you choose for your country that I did not think the comparison was well taken."

Because of Bentsen's failing health, I was not able to interview him about this exchange. But there was reporting afterward that Bentsen and his staff had noted that Quayle had previously compared himself with Kennedy. According to one of Bentsen's debate advisers, the "You're no Jack Kennedy" line had actually been discussed by Bentsen during the pre-debate preparation.

Bentsen himself, in a 1992 CNN interview, characterized his words as spontaneous. "Well, actually, it wasn't any prepared remark. It was just that, I finally was fed up with this comparison with Jack Kennedy. I just didn't think it was reality."

Later that year at a Senate news conference, he added this about his famous one-liner: "I wish now I had copyrighted it and was getting royalty on it."

In our documentary interview, Quayle said, "We actually had anticipated him using a line like that because during the campaign, if you recall, a lot of people, reporters, probably you, Jim, as well, said well, what kind of experience do you really have, and I would always make the factual reference to the experience that I had in the Congress and the Senate to the experience that Jack Kennedy had before he was elected president—a factual statement. . . . I was somewhat prepared for his line. It was a good line."

Did you feel it hurt you in the long run?

"Oh, in the long run, yes, because you guys keep running it over and over again. I'm sure you're going to run it again on this program, and it's not a good moment."

Quayle was right. We did run it on our documentary.

Ronald Reagan hit back at Bentsen on Quayle's behalf the morning after the debate in remarks to White House reporters.

"I thought that remark was a cheap shot and unbecoming a senator of the United States," said Reagan. "The only comparison [Quayle] was making was that he is being attacked, and I think unfairly, on the basis of his age and his experience in government, and he was pointing out that John Kennedy, who sought the highest office and won it, had actually less experience in government than he has and they were the same age."

Ed Fouhy, who had worked as an executive and/or producer at all three of the broadcast networks before joining the debate commission, added a couple of interesting postscripts to the Quayle-Bentsen debate.

Apparently, Bentsen barely knew Kennedy from when they served in the House together for five years in the late 1940s and early '50s. As Fouhy noted, if Quayle had known that, "he could have probably had a rejoinder: 'Well, now wait a minute, Senator, you didn't know [him], you just were in the House together.' They weren't close friends at all."

Fouhy also remembered what happened during Bentsen's pre-debate run-through at the hall in Omaha. The only people present that afternoon were a few technicians, a couple of Bentsen aides, and B.A. (for Beryl Ann), Bentsen's wife of forty-five years.

"When Bentsen finished his run-through, he was so relaxed and so full of himself, and thinking that this was going to be his night, that he picked her up, physically picked her up, and waltzed her around the stage with her feet off of the floor," Fouhy said. "He was ebullient about what was about to happen."

And that, remember, was *before* he'd gotten off his Kennedy line against Quayle.

CHAPTER 3

Apples and Apples

The campaign confrontations four years later in 1992 had a little bit of everything—and they made significant presidential debate history.

The then incumbent Republican president, George H. W. Bush, the Democratic nominee, Arkansas governor Bill Clinton, and Texas businessman Ross Perot, running as an independent, went at it three times within eight days that October.

The show-of-shows fourth act starred their running mates—Republican incumbent Dan Quayle, Democrat Al Gore, and independent James Stockdale.

These four debates marked the debut of the town hall and single-moderator formats, and much looser question and answer rules. They were also the first three-candidate debates ever.

Perot mostly avoided attacking Bush and Clinton directly during the debates, but the billionaire's folksy, rapid-fire quips added spice for everyone involved—including me and the other moderators.

"Look at all three of us. Decide who you think will do the job, pick that person in November because believe me, as I've said before, the party's over and it's time for the cleanup crew."

"I think it's a good time to face it in November. If they do, then they will have heard the harsh reality of what we have to do. I'm not playing Lawrence Welk music tonight—"

"I don't have any experience in running up a four-trillion-dollar debt. I don't have any experience in gridlock government, where nobody takes responsibility for anything and everybody blames everybody else."

The hottest debate exchanges came during the town hall debate in Richmond, Virginia, when Bush attacked Clinton for having protested against the Vietnam War while a student in Britain. But the Major Moment at that debate turned out to be sightings of Bush looking at his wristwatch. Later, in separate interviews, Clinton and Bush reflected on that moment.

"I saw him looking at his watch," Clinton said. "And I thought, I felt, when I saw it, that he was, you know, uncomfortable in that setting and wanted it to be over with. . . . But I think the reason so much was made of it is that the impression was forming that here was a very good man who was very devoted to our country but just didn't really believe that all these domestic issues should be dominating the way they were. . . . If someone had caught me or Ross Perot looking at our watch—unless it had been a bad moment in the debate—it probably wouldn't have resonated. But I think . . . the reason the watch thing hurt so badly was it tended to reinforce the problem he had in the election."

"You look at your watch and they say that he shouldn't have any business running for president," said Bush. "He's bored.

He's out of this thing, he's not with it and we need change. They took a little incident like that to show that I was, you know, out of it. They made a huge thing out of that. Now, was I glad when the damn thing was over? Yeah. And maybe that's why I was looking at it—only ten more minutes of this crap, I mean. Go ahead and use [that line]. I'm a free spirit now."

We used it.

The wristwatch incident aside, Clinton had been the major advocate of the town hall format, and he was delighted with how it went.

"I think presidents should be accountable to citizens, and I think it's very interesting the questions they ask and the way they ask them. Those folks who are out there trying to put lives together, and you know, pay bills, and send their kids to college, and deal with all the things that people deal with. And that's their perspective. It's the flesh and blood of America, so I love those things, and I loved that one. I think I did very well there."

Bush did not have a good time at Richmond. He didn't care much for the questions, particularly one from an audience member who challenged Bush for raising Clinton's having demonstrated against the Vietnam War as a character issue.

"What I didn't know is that beforehand they had rehearsed and identified some of the questioners and there was some guy that was, you know, so clearly . . . going to be antagonistic to me. . . . They singled him out to be the contentious questioner of George Bush. I mean that's, that's show business. Now should I have been able to react better and do a better job? I guess probably."

The moderator, Carole Simpson of ABC, had a very different take on what happened.

She recalled her relationship with the town hall audience—from selection to post-debate—in a 1994 conversation for the Washington Press Club Foundation's Women in Journalism oral history project.

"I said, 'Well, this is going to be really exciting, and I want you all to be loose. We're going to have fun. This is going to be great. We're making history and we're going to do it together. We're in this together—pals, buddies.' "

That's all she told the 209 Richmond-area uncommitted voters chosen to ask questions of Bush, Clinton, and Perot.

She said she was given little guidance about what each of the people might ask and, when the debate actually began, was told in her ear by Ed Fouhy, the debate executive producer, which people to call on.

Fouhy contended the selecting, done from what a pool director had put on the screen, was based solely on making sure all sections of the audience were equally represented. He vehemently denied Bush's charge that it had to do with whether a questioner was a specific kind of voter or pro or against any particular candidate.

He also said the questioners were not rehearsed or identified before the debate.

Fouhy got the impression during the afternoon run-through that Bush press secretary Marlin Fitzwater realized the danger zone Bush was about to enter. But it was too late to do anything about it.

Carole Simpson's handling of the ninety minutes became a

source of debate itself. Some thought she let it get too loose, and, as is the fate of all debate moderators now, partisans accused her of favoring one candidate over another. None of it got to her. She was comfortable with the job she did.

"It became a pretty important political event in the history of this country, and certainly in that election year," she said, "and I'm proud that I was part of it."

And Simpson, busy moderating, quite understandably did not even see President Bush glancing at his watch until afterward on the tape.

TWO DAYS EARLIER, Hal Bruno, ABC's political director, ran the Quayle-Gore-Stockdale event at Georgia Tech in Atlanta. The vice president, the senator, and the retired navy admiral debated in an open format that got to be a lot more open than originally intended.

Even the participants agreed afterward that it had elements of chaos—some called it an incoherent brawl.

Bruno opened the debate by explaining the groundbreaking rules: opening statements and from then on brief answers to questions, followed by five-minute discussions about each issue, with the candidates allowed to question one another directly.

Gore, standing at his podium across from Quayle with Stockdale in between, set the tone by welcoming Stockdale as a war hero and then saying to Quayle:

"And Mr. Vice President. Dan, if I may. . . . I'll make you a deal this evening. If you don't try to compare George Bush to Harry Truman, I won't compare you to Jack Kennedy."

That brought down the house.

Gore kept going, "Harry Truman."

Quayle broke in:

"Do you remember the last time someone compared themselves to Jack Kennedy? Do you remember what they said?"

Gore ignored that, continuing his sentence: "Harry Truman, it's worth remembering, assumed the presidency when Franklin Roosevelt died here in Georgia—only one of many occasions when fate thrust a vice president into the Oval Office at a time of crisis. It's something to think about during the debate this evening."

It wasn't long before Stockdale, in his opening statement, uttered his Major Moment line: "Who am I? Why am I here?"

That was followed a few minutes later with this freewheeling exchange.

STOCKDALE: Okay. I thought this was just an open session, this five-minute thing. I didn't have anything to add to his. But I will . . .

GORE: Well, I'll jump in if you don't want—

QUAYLE: I thought anyone could jump in whenever they wanted to.

BRUNO: Okay, whatever pleases you gentlemen is fine with me. You're the candidates.

QUAYLE: But I want Admiral Stockdale's time.

BRUNO: This is not the Senate, where you can trade off time. Go ahead, Senator Gore.

GORE: I'll let you all figure out the rules, I've got some points that I want to make here and I still haven't gotten an answer to my question on when you guys are going to start worrying about this country, but I want to elaborate on it before—

QUAYLE: Why doesn't the Democratic Congress— why doesn't Democratic the Congress—

BRUNO: Mr. Vice President, let him say his thoughts, and then you can come in.

GORE: I was very patient in letting you get off that string of attacks. We've been listening to—

QUAYLE: Good points.

GORE:—trickle-down economics for twelve years now, and you all still support trickle-down to the very last drop. And, you know, talking about this point of concentrating on every other country in the world as opposed to the people of our country right here at home . . .

QUAYLE: Well, we're going to have plenty of time to talk about trickle-down government, which you're for. But the question—

GORE: Well, I'd like to hear the answer.

QUAYLE: But the question is—the question is—and which you have failed to address, and that is, why is Bill Clinton qualified to be president of the United States. You've talked about—

GORE: Oh, I'll be happy to answer that question—

QUAYLE: You've talked about Jim Baker. You've talked about trickle-down economics. You've talked about the worst economy—

BRUNO: Now, wait a minute. The question was about—

QUAYLE: —in fifty years.

GORE: I'll be happy to answer those. May I answer—

QUAYLE: Why is he qualified to be president of the United States?

GORE: I'll be happy to—

QUAYLE: I want to go back and make a point—

GORE: Well, you've asked me the question. If you won't answer my question I will answer yours.

QUAYLE: I have not asked you a question. I've made a statement, in that you have not told us why Bill Clinton is qualified to be president of the United States. I pointed out what he said about the Persian Gulf War. But let me repeat for you. Here's what he said, Senator. You know full well what he said.

GORE: You want me to answer your question?

QUAYLE: I'm making a statement. Then you can answer it.

BRUNO: Can we give Admiral Stockdale a chance to come in, please—

There was a lot of talk at once among everyone on the stage. Then:

QUAYLE: [*inaudible*] Here's what he said. I mean, this is the Persian Gulf War—the most important event in his political lifetime and here's what Bill Clinton says. "If it's a close vote, I'd vote with the majority."

BRUNO: Let's give Admiral Stockdale a chance to come in.

QUAYLE: But he was the minority. That qualifies you for being president of the United States? I hope America is listening very closely to this debate tonight.

STOCKDALE: And I think America is seeing right now the reason this nation is in gridlock.

The audience in the Atlanta hall hooted and hollered as they had many times from the beginning of the debate, including when Stockdale uttered his famous line, "Who am I? Why am I here?" Bruno had tried to keep the audience silent but to no avail.

Stockdale wasn't laughing when I talked to him seven years later in a hotel room in Los Angeles.

"I never got back to that because there was never an opportunity for me to explain my life to people," he said. "It was so different from Quayle and Gore."

Stockdale was a career navy man, a fighter pilot who was shot down over North Vietnam in 1965, taken prisoner, and withstood severe torture and starvation. As the senior officer, Stockdale created a prison system that allowed the captured Americans to communicate with one another. He received the Medal of Honor for his actions, rose to the rank of vice admiral, and served as president of the Naval War College.

"The four years in solitary confinement in Vietnam, seven and a half years in prisons, [dropping] the first bomb that started the . . . American bombing raid in . . . North Vietnam," Stockdale said. "I don't say it just to brag, but, I mean, my sensitivities are completely different."

As Quayle and Gore went at each other, Stockdale, from another world, mostly remained a spectator. At one point, Bruno broke in to give Stockdale a chance to speak, and the admiral said, "I would like to get in. I feel like I'm an observer at a Ping-Pong game."

Stockdale expanded on that later.

"The whole thing reminded me of a Maypole dance. I was standing there trying to figure out how I could get my oar in and never really did. And they're just exercising right where they live every day. They'll take an issue like Medicare, and they'll go from this way to that, and there's four different ways you can look at it, and they dance counterclockwise awhile. I said, what am I doing here? How can I break in and tell them . . . that's not the whole story on being the national leader."

Stockdale drew understanding and sympathy from voters who watched the debate but also criticism for a lack of knowledge of the issues.

Guilty as charged, the admiral said to me. "That's a fair criticism, but I didn't get much help from anybody about it."

Then he told this story:

"Sybil [his wife] said to me . . . 'Are you going to have to be in that—if they have a VP debate'—and it hadn't been really decided yet—'You're not going to have to be in that, are you?' I said, 'No, everybody knows I'm not a politician.' . . . And about a week before the debate I called Ross [Perot]. I seldom called him, but in this case I said, 'You know, I'm in luck. Nobody has ever mentioned that debate, and it's too late to invite me, and I think that's as it ought to be because I'm not a politician.'

"He said, 'Oh, Jim, I forgot to tell you. Your invitation came here about three weeks ago and we accepted for you, and I forgot to tell you.' So that was the preparation."

There were definitely no briefing books and, more important, no pre-debate discussion with Perot.

"I never had a single conversation about politics with Ross Perot in my life; still haven't."

I asked Quayle if Stockdale was a distraction.

"I wouldn't use the word 'distraction,' but it was more difficult to continue to focus on Clinton and Gore with Admiral Stockdale there, because I didn't want to talk about Perot. We were really just trying to forget about Ross Perot, and so therefore I would just as soon him not have been on the stage."

On *Larry King Live* right after the debate, a caller asked Perot how he could defend selecting Stockdale as a running mate. Perot said, "I don't know what your concerns are. If your concerns are that he is not a glib talker in a debate setting, then possibly that's your concerns. I'm sure you know that he is a hero's hero. He is a Medal of Honor winner. He is a man that nobody could break under terrible conditions. He is also a scholar. He is a brilliant man."

Comparing him to Quayle and Gore, Perot said, "They'd have trouble getting a job in the private sector. They don't have any experience. They're nice guys but they—you know, you wouldn't hire them as pilots. They don't know how to fly. You wouldn't hire them as businessmen."

Hal Bruno said he went into that debate determined to make sure everyone was treated fairly but basically played the role of a "potted plant because nobody was tuning in to hear me."

He described what happened:

"Gore and Quayle just absolutely took off on each other, Quayle was attacking Clinton through Gore. Gore picked up on it and came back savagely—really came back savagely. Quayle was the same way. Stockdale stood there and just watched."

Hal realized that he had to do something or it would spin even further out of control. "I had to many times, just stop it and say you can't do that. And, boy, every chance they got they just turned loose on each other."

He thought Stockdale was out of his element.

"He was a wonderful man—just a tremendous person. He was always laughed at for saying 'Who am I and why am I here' when all that was was a lead-in—in his opening statement—to something that was a very sensitive and brilliant discourse on how he felt about the electoral system and so on."

Very few listeners in the hall or anywhere else seem to have heard the rest of what James Stockdale said that night:

Who am I? Why am I here? I'm not a politician—everybody knows that. So don't expect me to use the language of the Washington insider. Thirty-seven years in the navy, and only one of them up there in Washington. And now I'm an academic. The centerpiece of my life was the Vietnam War. I was there the day it started. I led the first bombing raid against North Vietnam. I was there the day it ended, and I was there for everything in between. Ten years in Vietnam, aerial combat, and torture. I know some things about the Vietnam War better than anybody in the world. I know some things about the Vietnam War better than anybody in the world.

And I know how governments, how American governments can be—can be courageous, and how they can be callow. And that's important. That's one thing I'm an insider on.

I was the leader of the underground of the American pilots who were shot down in prison in North Vietnam. You should know that the American character displayed in those dungeons by those fine men was a thing of beauty.

I look back on those years as the beginning of wisdom, learning everything a man can learn about the vulnerabilities and the strengths that are ours as Americans.

Why am I here tonight? I am here because I have in my brain and in my heart what it takes to lead America through tough times.

Hal Bruno recalled that at one point in the raucous debate Stockdale had trouble with his hearing aid, and he began fumbling around with it because he couldn't hear what was being said.

"I almost blurted out to Stockdale 'You may be the luckiest man in America.' "

A FURTHER FORMAT experiment was at the heart of the final 1992 presidential debate in East Lansing, Michigan. The first half of those ninety minutes had a sole moderator—me—asking questions of George H. W. Bush, Bill Clinton, and Ross Perot with no formal restraints on answer times or subjects. Three panelists would then revert to the traditional format in the second half.

The Quayle-Gore-Stockdale affair and the Richmond town hall excitements had focused anxious attention on everyone involved in preparing for East Lansing—me in particular.

I decided the key was the opening question for each of the candidates. I worked hard on them, based on a theme I would state as a preface to Bush, Perot, and Clinton at the beginning of the debate.

Just before leaving the East Lansing hotel for the debate, I called my wife, Kate, to run it all by her. A novelist, she was in Washington for a book event, unable to hold my hand in East Lansing. I read her my preface:

"It seems, from what some voters said at your Richmond debate, and from polling and other data, that each of you, fairly or not, faces serious voter concerns about the underlying credibility and believability of what each of you says you would do as president in the next four years."

I then read her the three questions—one for each.

There was absolute silence.

Not too sweetly, I asked her what the problem was.

"You've got two apples and one orange," she replied, and quickly explained her opinion.

I snapped back something about the Secret Service having said it was time to go and hung up.

Kate was well aware by now of how I moved into a zone-out

state as any particular debate approached. I closed down my mind to all outside "things," with the hope that I could float as if in space to and through the debate. Her apples-oranges point had stopped the zoning.

In the ride to the debate hall—Wharton Center at Michigan State University—there were two interventions. First, my annoyance with Kate settled down enough for me to realize that she was right. Second, a long freight train halted our two-car moderator/panelist motorcade for several minutes, giving me time to come up with another apple to replace that wayward orange.

Minutes later at the Wharton Center, I tried to call her from a phone in the small backstage holding area to tell her how grateful I was. There was no answer.

She told me afterward that her distress over having ruined my zone-out just before the debate had driven her out of the house for a quick, nervous neighborhood walk with Amanda, our youngest daughter.

With the president, the governor, and the businessman at their podiums and me sitting at a small table facing them, the debate began.

I started with my apple for Clinton.

"Governor Clinton, in accordance with the draw, those concerns about you are first: You are promising to create jobs, reduce the deficit, reform the health care system, rebuild the infrastructure, guarantee college education for everyone who is qualified, among other things, all with financial pain only for the very rich. Some people are having trouble apparently believing that is possible.

"Should they have that concern?"

Clinton responded that he could do it all, but both Bush and Perot underlined the public's doubts.

I went on to my apple for Bush:

"Mr. President, let's move to some of the leadership concerns that have been voiced about you. And they relate to something you said in your closing statement in Richmond the other night about the president being the manager of crises. And that relates to an earlier criticism, that you began to focus on the economy, on health care, on racial divisions in this country, only after they became crises.

"Is that a fair criticism?"

Bush said he didn't think it was fair at all. Perot said he had come to talk about issues, not the individuals. But Clinton went back and forth with Bush over the crises issue.

As I let that two-way play out, I felt Perot storm clouds forming. In his distinctive high-pitched voice, he pushed me:

"I thought you had forgotten I was here."

Perot was smiling—almost—but his body language made it clear I had better call on him soon to say what he had come to say or there was going to be trouble. He would, most likely, publicly charge that I was not treating him fairly.

But I held up a hand as if to say, "In a minute, Ross"—a kind of respectful use of body language, as I saw it—and kept the Bush-Clinton exchange going another minute or so before saying:

"I have to let—we have to talk about Ross Perot now, or he'll get me."

And I finally tossed Perot the apple question I had for him. Unfortunately it came out ungrammatical, awkward—and much too long. My face warms to read it even now in cold print.

"Mr. Perot, on this issue that I raised at the very beginning and we've been talking about, which is leadership, as president of the United States, it concerns—my reading of it, at least—my concerns about you, as expressed by folks in the polls and other places, it goes like this: You had a problem with General Motors. You took your seven hundred and fifty million dollars and you left. You had a problem in the spring and summer about some personal hits you took as a potential candidate for president of the United States and you walked out.

"Does that say anything relevant to how you would function as president of the United States?"

Perot came back with a punch saying he sold his General Motors stock because the people running it were brain-dead. In another health analogy he said:

"If you have a heart problem, you don't wait till a heart attack to address it."

The "personal hits" referred to a charge that the Bush campaign was allegedly planning to sabotage the upcoming wedding of Perot's daughter with some kind of embarrassing photograph. Perot gave that as a reason for suspending his presidential campaign in July while ahead of both Bush and Clinton in the polls.

The "quitter" charge followed him when he returned to the race three months later.

Perot finished his answer to my apple this way:

"Now what happened in July we've covered again and again and again. But I think in terms of the American people's concern about my commitment, I'm here tonight, folks. . . . And talk about not quitting. I'm spending my money on this campaign; the two parties are spending your money, taxpayer money. I put my wallet on the table for you and your children."

Clinton, when I asked for his response, said, after a few preliminaries:

"I have no criticism of Mr. Perot."

Bush ended his answer with:

"My argument is not with Ross Perot. It is more with Governor Clinton."

And the storm passed over me—and all.

THE ONLY GENERAL comment from Perot on the debates was what he said later on *Larry King*.

He did no "debate prep" except go to the barbershop.

"We were just sitting there in the barbershop, and we talked about what the issues were that concerned people in the barbershop—literally, got my hair cut, got on the airplane, and I was ready for the debate."

I have always believed that Ross Perot's decision not to participate in our *Debating Our Destiny* interviews was based, at least partly, on what I did to him in *The Last Debate*, my novel that was published in 1995.

In that 100 percent piece of fiction, "Perot" is the host of *Sunday Morning Ross*, which is exactly what the title suggests—a Sunday morning television network talk show, à la the real

Face the Nation, Meet the Press, and *This Week*. There are references to "Perot" and his weekly program throughout the novel.

But then, as the plot goes, "Perot" is replaced by two young journalists who had become stars for what they did as debate panelists. His firing prompts "Perot" to ignore his promise to go quietly and, instead, on his last broadcast he makes a valedictory "squeaky, fiery speech about the awfulness of the people who run the ABS television network and all of network television." He talks for twenty-two minutes directly to the camera and then storms off the set.

Among his parting lines: "I've been asked if I might hit back by buying this network. Forget it, friends. I've got a lot better things to do with my money—which, by the way, I didn't get by investing in the dying and the past. . . .

"These people aren't long for this world. I understand a merger with the Disney Channel is in the works. Makes perfect sense. One Mickey Mouse outfit deserves another."

Later, at a news conference in the ABS News Washington bureau parking lot, "Perot" adds:

"These people aren't qualified to run a toilet concession at a roadside park on the information superhighway."

I had known Ross Perot—the real one—for years, going back to my reporting days in Texas. He felt that I had abused that long, friendly relationship by making fun of him in the novel. Direct as ever, he let me have it in an angry phone call right after the book was published. In retrospect, I think he had a right to be annoyed. I should never have used his real name the way I did in a work of fiction.

I wish I had given him the name of a Dallas Cowboy football player, as I did most of the other characters.

My path did not cross Perot's again until October 2009 when we both attended a fund-raising gala for the Dallas Public Library. There we had a pleasant exchange, almost like old prenovel times.

I put in a quick new pitch for an opportunity to talk to him—for this book—about the 1992 debates. I reminded him that they were important to the history of presidential debates, with their innovative town hall and sole moderator formats and first attempts at opening up the rules. He gave me his card with his Dallas phone number.

Three days later, from my office back in Washington, I followed up and, within minutes, Perot was on the line. I repeated the pitch, adding the names of the former presidents, vice presidents, and other candidates I had already spoken with.

"I have nothing to say about all of that," Perot said.

I made a second pass and he said, again, "I just have nothing to say."

I pressed on with a question about what James Stockdale had told me about having had no real conversation with him about the debates, positions, issues, or anything else concerning politics.

"I don't have any memory of any of that," Perot said.

"Memory of having had a conversation at all or what was said?" I persisted.

"I really do not want to talk about any of this," he said one more time.

And that was—is—that.

I did do one constructive thing shortly after hanging up. I wrote a note to Perot, thanking him for taking my call and then apologizing for what I had written in *The Last Debate* fourteen years before.

I wish I had done it long ago.

IF I HAD had a full chance to talk to Perot, I would have also asked about his remarkable non-presidential NAFTA debate with Al Gore on November 9, 1993.

That ninety minutes on CNN was a major event in the history of televised debates as well as in the national controversy about the North American Free Trade Agreement that finally ended with its passage by Congress.

In the pre-debate chatter, Perot's folksiness was given the edge over Gore's stiffness.

They sat side by side in a Washington television studio across the table from Larry King, the moderator. Gore, then vice president under President Clinton, supported Senate ratification of the treaty; Perot was vehemently opposed.

King laid out the wide-open rules of the debate at the beginning: no formal statement-and-rebuttal format and no time limits on questions or answers.

After giving out the telephone numbers for viewers to call in, he said, "We're going to wing back and forth, and then include your phone calls."

Afterward, there was near unanimity from the pundits and polls that Gore got the better of Perot that night. Words like "crushed," "annihilated," "destroyed," and "demolished" were used in stories after the debate, which had a still-standing cable TV record audience of eleven million. Much fun was made of Perot for his constant call to Gore, "Let me finish."

King, the moderator, drew criticism for the way he handled the evening. Howard Rosenberg, the Pulitzer Prize–winning TV critic of the *Los Angeles Times,* landed the toughest hits. They came under the headline:

REAL LOSER IN AL GORE VS. ROSS PEROT: LARRY KING.

Rosenberg even jumped King for calling the combatants by their first names, "Ross" and "Al," but the main complaint was about his passivity—for being what Rosenberg called an "absent" moderator.

I think Rosenberg's hits were off the mark—and unfair. King did exactly what a moderator should do—leave it to the combatants and stay out of it as much as possible. Absent is sometimes the best thing to be.

A persistent Gore charge that frustrated King and brought Perot to his testiest was the money behind the lobbying effort against NAFTA ratification. Gore said Perot had spent more against it than those supporting it.

PEROT: That is not even close to the truth. It is a matter of record how much Mexico has spent. It is a matter of record how much USA/NAFTA has spent. You take—

GORE: Why isn't it a matter of record—

PEROT: I, I—

GORE: —how much you all spent? Can that be a matter of public record? Can you release those numbers?

PEROT: I really would appreciate being able to speak.

KING: All right, go ahead, it was a question he raised before—

PEROT: I really would—

GORE: It's a fair question, isn't it?

PEROT: Excuse me—

GORE: I raised it earlier.

PEROT: It was my understanding tonight we'd have a format where you would ask the questions.

KING: Okay.

PEROT: I would be able—I am not able to finish.

KING: But if he makes a statement—I'm just trying to balance so that he answers yours—

PEROT: Well, excuse me, I would like—I would like to finish a sentence, just once before the program's over. Now, we are not able to buy time. If you are anti-NAFTA, you cannot buy time on the networks. We have had to go buy local station time. We cannot buy network time because the networks won't sell it. That's the covers on how much you're spending. We didn't run ten-page supplements in *The New York Times,* et cetera, et cetera.

GORE: Okay, now, I'd like to respond to that, okay?

KING: Let him finish, he's got one more thing.

GORE: All right, go ahead. I do want to respond.

Then a few moments later, Perot tried to move on to NAFTA's effect on manufacturing, arguing that the United States would not be able to sell goods to Mexican citizens who made low wages. Gore seemed to ignore his assertion.

GORE: Okay. First of all, you will notice, and the audience will notice, that he does not want to publicly release how much money he's spending, how much money he's received from other sources to campaign against NAFTA. I would like to see those public releases that the other side has made. Now, let me come to the point—he talked about accuracy of forecasts and numbers. I watched on this program, right here at this desk, when the war against Iraq was about to take place, and you told Larry King, "This is a terrible mistake because it will lead to the death of forty thousand American troops." You said you had talked to the person who had "ordered the caskets." You were wrong about that. You said on *Larry King* just before the election that after Election Day, there would be one hundred banks that would fail, costing the taxpayers one hundred billion dollars. You were wrong about that. Now, the politics of negativism and fear only go so far.

KING: All right—

Then, much later after two commercial breaks, King reminded Perot that he still had not answered Gore's questions about the financing of the anti-NAFTA campaign.

PEROT: Okay, fine, I'll answer it. See, again, he throws up propaganda. He throws up gorilla dust that makes no sense.

KING: What is it then?

PEROT: May I finish?

KING: Yeah.

PEROT: Okay. Most of the television time I bought during the [1992 Perot-Stockdale presidential] campaign. That is a matter of public record. I have had two television shows since the campaign in the spring. They cost about four hundred thousand dollars apiece. Those were network shows. Then we just did a NAFTA show, but we have to buy the time locally. I don't have the figures yet on what that cost me or I'd be glad to tell you.

KING: You're spending—

PEROT: I had to buy—no, I buy the television time because I don't want to take the members' [of Perot's anti-NAFTA organization] money for that. They understand that, they approve of that.

GORE: Can I—it's not all his money, and we don't know because they do not—

PEROT: No, but television time. I just told you.

GORE: Well, but—see, they do not release the records, but I accept your response because you have said that now—

PEROT: If it makes you feel better to see the checks and the bills from the network—

GORE: It's okay for you to interrupt but not me?

KING: Okay, all right—

GORE: Now, hold on. You just said that you would—

KING: Let's go back to jobs.

GORE: You just said that you would release the records, and I appreciate that. Now, this—

PEROT: It has nothing to do with what's going to happen to our country.

GORE: Well, we need to know who's trying to influence it.

PEROT: I am paying for it, it's that simple.

KING: We got the answer.

Ross Perot made another run for president in 1996 as a candidate of the Reform Party, but his performance against Gore during the NAFTA debate was among the reasons it did not go as far as in 1992. The Commission on Presidential Debates ruled that he was too low in the public opinion polls to qualify for joining the presidential debates between President Clinton and Republican Bob Dole.

Perot ended up drawing 8 percent of the popular vote in 1996, compared to the 19 percent he had received four years earlier. Many in politics—particularly George H. W. Bush and his supporters—believe Perot's 19 percent was a major factor in the final outcome of the 1992 election. Clinton won 44 percent to Bush's 37 percent, but what if there had been no Perot—no third candidate? In a straight two-way race, isn't it more likely Bush would have won more of those Perot-minded voters than Clinton? And thus Bush would have won reelection and there might never have been a Bill Clinton presidency?

There has been a marked absence of Ross Perot from politics and view since 1996. Whatever his stylistic quirks, he deserves to be remembered as a man of substance who used his own money and iconoclastic words to spark serious discourse about things that mattered.

CHAPTER 4

Personal Differences

Whatever else, the Perot-less debates of 1996 were a big deal for me, because I moderated all three of them—something that had never happened before.

I had initially received a simpler telephoned invitation from Janet Brown of the debate commission. She asked if I would do the first debate between President Clinton and his Republican opponent, Senator Bob Dole, in Hartford, Connecticut, on October 6, 1996—barely a week later.

I hadn't even gone into high-nerves mode about that when there came a back-channel call a short while later.

"If asked, would you also do the other presidential and the Gore-Kemp vice presidential one, too?"

That was from Les Crystal, *The NewsHour*'s executive producer. He reported that the two campaigns were hopelessly deadlocked over who was acceptable to moderate those debates. "They've already agreed on you to do the first one, so in order to end the arguing and get on with it . . ."

Otherwise, the 1996 debates were remembered mostly for what did *not* happen. No one, including the Republican nominees Bob Dole and Jack Kemp, went after Clinton on the so-called character issue—a code phrase for the Women Problem.

As moderator, I did toss a few neutral opportunities that way, but nobody caught them.

The Hartford debate at the Bushnell theater was a podium event with strict rules: two-minute opening statements, ninety-second answers, sixty-second rebuttals, thirty-second responses, and two-minute closing statements.

That buttoned-up game plan was insisted on, I was told, by the Dole campaign. They wanted to play to Dole's strength as a quick-wit short responder and away from Clinton's as a voluble, long-form charmer. The trade-off was Dole agreeing—at Clinton's insistence—that the second debate would be a town hall format.

As Hartford approached, Dole was down twenty points in the polls. It was now or never for the former World War II hero and U.S. Senate leader from Kansas. He either went for broke against Clinton in Hartford at their first debate, or the 1996 presidential election was over.

My own preparations centered on the belief that if Dole was going to do something that mattered it had to happen in the first twenty minutes to hold the big national television audience.

This was pre–Monica Lewinsky but there was already much in the public discourse about Clinton's alleged womanizing, especially related to a twelve-year affair with a singer/actress named Gennifer Flowers.

I assumed that if Dole tried to break things open, he would use it.

I also thought it was possible that Dole, with nothing to lose, could declare right at the beginning of the debate that what he had to say could not be said in structured short chunks. Let's forget the rules and go at it one-on-one and have a real bloodletting.

If such a thing occurred, I planned to let it play out for a few minutes, then I would stop the debate and announce to the candidates that I would—right there—help negotiate a new set of rules.

My trek toward a zone-out state about it included imagining—literally, word for word—what I would say, how Dole and Clinton would each respond. . . .

Nothing happened. The debate proceeded quietly, routinely for the first twenty minutes and beyond about tort reform, Social Security, taxes, the deficit, drugs, and guns. There were no fireworks, not even any sparklers.

It was time for me as the moderator to shake things up.

More than fifty minutes in, I finally asked Dole: "Senator Dole, we've talked mostly now about differences between the two of you that relate to policy, issues, and that sort of thing. Are there also significant differences in the more personal area that are relevant to this election?"

Dole answered with a comment about tax cuts, economic reform, and how he thought the government could do better.

Then he asked, as if to confirm my original question, "Are there personal differences?"

Yes, I said, that are relevant to the election.

DOLE: Well, my blood pressure's lower, my weight, my cholesterol. But I will not make health an issue in this campaign. So—I think he's a bit taller than I am. But I think there are personal differences. I mean . . . I don't like to get into personal matters. As far as I'm concerned, this is a campaign about issues.

And that was about it—not only the debate but, maybe, the election.

What I did not know at the time was that *The Washington Post* and other news organizations were working on a story about an alleged adulterous affair Dole had had twenty-eight years before while he was married to his first wife.

If I had known about it, would I have asked Dole about it during the debate?

No. Not until—and unless—it had been reported in the credible public press. Or Clinton himself had brought it up.

Making such a decision would have been a perfect example of the walk down a knife blade that goes with being a moderator—presidential and all other kinds.

THAT DOLE STORY still had not been reported two days later when I gave the Dole campaign a second chance to engage the Clinton character issue.

It occurred at the beginning of the October 9, 1996, vice presidential debate between the Democratic incumbent Al Gore and Jack Kemp, a former Republican congressman and pro football quarterback, at the Bayfront Center in St. Petersburg, Florida.

LEHRER: Some supporters of Senator Dole have expressed disappointment over his unwillingness in Hartford Sunday night to draw personal and ethical differences between him and President Clinton. How do you feel about it?

Kemp, inexplicably, seemed unprepared for what, according to every preview story in the press, would be a first question along those lines.

KEMP: Wow, in ninety seconds? I can't clear my throat in ninety seconds. Jim, Bob Dole and myself do not see Al Gore and Bill Clinton as our enemy. We see them as our opponents.

This is the greatest democracy in the world. People are watching not only throughout this country, but all over the world as to how this democracy can function with civility and respect, and decency and integrity. Bob Dole is one of those men who served in the United States Senate; his public life is a public record. He fought on the battlefield. He has worked with Democrats and Republicans. In my opinion, it is beneath Bob Dole to go after anyone personally. Clearly, Abraham Lincoln put it best when he said you serve your party best by serving the nation first. And I can't think of a better way of serving this nation in 1996 than by electing Bob Dole as the president of the United States of America. These issues are fully capable of being understood and reflected upon by the

American people. This is a democracy in which we have the freest press and the greatest First Amendment rights in the history of mankind. And Bob and I respect that. These issues will be aired, but they'll be aired with dignity and respect, and, ultimately, leave it to the American people to make up their minds about who should be the leader of this country into the twenty-first century.

LEHRER: Mr. Vice President?

GORE: Thank you, Mr. Lehrer. And I would like to thank the people of St. Petersburg for being such wonderful hosts. My family and I are very glad to be here and I would like to thank Jack Kemp for the answer that he just gave. I think we have an opportunity tonight to have a positive debate about this country's future. I'd like to start by offering you a deal, Jack. If you won't use any football stories, I won't tell any of my warm and humorous stories about chlorofluorocarbon abatement.

KEMP: It's a deal. I can't even pronounce it.

GORE: What I do want to talk about tonight is Bill Clinton's positive plan for America's future. . . .

Again, so much for the character issue.

There is no evidence that the election result would have been any different had Dole—or I or anyone else—concentrated on Clinton's personal problems in the 1996 debates.

Presidential debate historian Sidney Kraus of Cleveland State University added a PS to my own Gore-Kemp experience. In his book *Televised Presidential Debates and Public Policy,* he noted that I had not had a "sweet day" because "Lehrer had five uncomfortable experiences."

Kraus cited a story in the *St. Petersburg Times* that reported Secret Service and dressing room problems, a too-small desk on the set for my various papers, a buzzing earpiece, and a crashing computer on which I was writing debate questions.

"Having had such a disappointing day, it must have been his easy-going manner that allowed him to go on and moderate the debate without a hitch," Kraus concluded graciously.

My Secret Service discomfort actually began at the Clinton-Dole event in Hartford three days earlier.

I was placed in a tiny holding room next to the men's room in the basement of the Bushnell theater—alone—for almost two hours before debate time. I was told all other space in the building was reserved for the candidates and their campaign staffs. So be it.

Finally, with less than fifteen minutes to go, I was taken into another tiny basement room nearby for makeup. A technician came and told me to remove my coat and the security passes that hung over my neck so I could be fitted with a wireless microphone. I put the passes in my coat pocket and returned to my cubbyhole.

Then, Les Crystal, *The NewsHour*'s executive producer and my chief debate helper, and I went up a flight of stairs for the debate. Crystal was holding my coat for me as we walked. There were now less than five minutes to go before I was to be introduced to the audience and get the show on the road.

We arrived at the top of the stairs behind the curtains on the left wing of the stage, only a few feet from where it would all happen.

"Stop!" said a young man with an earpiece in his ear and a bulge on his right hip under his suit coat. He stepped in front of me and blocked my way with his body. Clearly he was an agent of the U.S. Secret Service.

"Where is your ID—your security badge?" he demanded. His voice was tight, his eyes were lit.

"I've got it in my coat pocket, which is right over there—"

He made a move that, in my agitated state, seemed to be step one toward my being grabbed and maybe thrown to the ground and handcuffed.

"I'm the moderator!" I shouted like an angry child and pointed to a spot through the curtains less than ten feet away. "There are three people who have to be out there on the stage, and I am one of them!"

Crystal kept saying, "He's the moderator, he's the moderator," as he desperately tried to fish my credentials out of my coat.

Two other earpieced men appeared at my front and back. They seemed to know who I was and why I was backstage.

With only seconds to go for a few settle-down breaths, I was finally allowed to proceed to my desk and moderate a debate aimed at resolving who should be the next leader of the Free World.

A high-ranking Secret Service official later called and apologized to me and promised nothing like that would happen again. And since I still had two more debates to go, he said photos of me would be provided to all agents involved.

And then I went off to St. Petersburg to do the Kemp-Gore debate seventy-two hours later.

Guess what? While being taken on a run-through by debate commission staff that first afternoon, I was locked out of the Bayfront Center. A Secret Service agent on the door refused me permission to re-enter. My security badge was the wrong color—or something. It took a very loud call to a supervisor somewhere in bureaucracy-land to get me back inside.

Clearly, in the world of profiling, among other handicaps, I did not look like a presidential debate moderator, at least to two pairs of U.S. Secret Service eyes.

Fortunately, Mike Brewer, husband of Janet Brown and a debate commission volunteer, among many other wonderful things, made it all better—and fun. He somehow talked the St. Petersburg police into providing a flashing-lights motorcycle escort for my limo ride from the hotel to the Bayfront Center the next evening for the debate itself. The distance was barely a city block.

A phalanx of smiling Secret Service agents escorted me into the hall and directly through security without even a cursory check. (This was pre-9/11.)

I was taken to my very own personal holding area, which was the size of a large hotel ballroom and fully stocked with snacks and drinks galore.

FROM ST. PETERSBURG I went immediately to San Diego, California, for the second Clinton-Dole main event. It was to be in the so-called town hall format.

And I use "so-called" deliberately.

Many of those exercises do not remotely resemble the original town hall meetings that began in early New England. Residents would assemble at prescribed times and places to publicly exchange views on how their town should be governed and to question those in charge. In a few towns, votes were taken that were binding, but mostly the meetings provided an opportunity for talking, asking, and answering.

That purpose remains, but, through the years, the term "town hall meeting" has come to mean different things.

For some, it is a mob scene with people shouting down speakers, as happened during the anti-Vietnam events of the 1960s and, more recently, when members of Congress came home to their districts to discuss health care reform in the summer of 2009.

For others, a town hall meeting is a partisan way to stage an appearance of public questioning with attendance limited to only those who agree with the speaker/politician/premise.

For still others, it is a way to get seemingly "ordinary" people with varying views to question a political or other kind of public figure with prepared and prescreened questions, mostly for the benefit of television. In fact, some are staged almost solely for television purposes and more closely resemble game shows than real town hall meetings.

Some, I regret to say, are also obviously designed as platforms for TV news personalities to ask their own questions or show their stuff, rather than trigger serious dialogue.

The first time any kind of town hall format was used in a presidential debate was the 1992 Richmond event moderated by Carole Simpson. Bill Clinton, through his campaign negotiators, pushed hard for it to be the format for one of the three debates, but Ed Fouhy told me that, surprisingly, the representatives of George H. W. Bush—mistakenly, it turned out—favored it as well.

Because of his polling numbers, Perot was brought into those debates after they were set and was not involved in any of the debate negotiations, including the selection of formats.

The 1996 town hall event was at the Shiley Theater on the campus of the University of San Diego. Some 113 people representing a cross section of the San Diego area, selected and screened for the debate commission by the Gallup organization to be "uncommitted," would ask the questions.

Just before the event, I gave them a brief procedures rundown and a polite sermon about no speeches, please, questions only—the shorter the better. I also told them the time restraints and rules were such that no more than about 20 of the 113 were actually going to get an opportunity to ask a question.

I expanded on my instructions in the "good evening" opening to the debate itself:

They [the citizens] were told to come tonight with questions. Nobody from the debate commission or the two campaigns has any idea what those questions are. Neither do I. We will all be hearing them for the first time at the same time. I met with this group three hours ago, and we spoke only about how it was going to work tonight. They are sitting in five sections. I will call on individuals at random, moving from one section to another with each new question, alternating the questions between the two candidates.

After opening statements from Dole and Clinton, the first difficult moments came when I realized that, no matter what, I had to make sure there was a good race, age, and gender mix in the questioners.

With that in mind, I scanned the audience sitting in the bleachers that circled the two candidates and me, and I began calling on people.

Uniting the country was the first topic, followed by health care. A soldier/small business owner asked about the gap between military and civilian pay scales. A man challenged a Dole statement that nicotine was not addictive. There were questions about funding Medicare, reforming welfare, and reducing capital gains taxes.

Then came a zinger for Dole from a college student.

"All the controversy regarding your age, how do you feel you can respond to young voices of America today and tomorrow?"

Dole responded.

"Well, I think age is very—you know, wisdom comes with age, experience, and intelligence. And if you have some of each—and I have some age, some experience, and some intelligence—that adds up to wisdom. . . ."

Clinton one-upped him.

"I can only tell you that I don't think Senator Dole is too old to be president. It's the age of his ideas that I question. . . ."

Nearing the end, I realized after the seventeenth question

that all but one on the Middle East had been about domestic issues. I asked if anybody had another foreign affairs question.

That brought a concern about how to deal with Japan's trade deficit.

Then came the last two questions—one was about the responsibility of the president to inspire young people; the other was on gay rights.

After the closing statements I thanked everyone, said good night, and felt as if I had at least dodged another moderating bullet.

Dole and Clinton had both done all right and, on the most important scoring column, neither had made any game-changing mistakes.

Clinton went in still way ahead of Dole and came out the same.

BOTH BILL CLINTON and Bob Dole talked fully and openly about their debates.

I sat down with Clinton at the Oval Office in August 2000, five months before he left the White House. He spoke with delight and detail about his experiences, almost like a football star going back over some of his big plays, but from the coach's as well as a player's point of view. Here was a master politician talking shop.

Bob Dole was just as forthcoming when I spoke with him at his downtown Washington office in November 1999.

He revealed that there was considerable discussion within his campaign about whether to get into what he called "the character thing" and, if so, how far to go. "I decided not to do that, even though I was being pushed by some. I said, well, you get into that, I think everybody loses. That was my view."

I wondered whether Clinton had been expecting Dole to go after him on character issues—particularly after I gave Dole an opportunity to do so halfway through the first debate in Hartford.

"Oh, yes," answered Clinton, adding that he was most surprised Dole did not hit him harder.

I did not press Dole on what effect, if any, the possibility of a news story about his long-ago affair may have had. Apparently, according to the public record, nobody else ever did either.

I did ask about his polling numbers: "When you went into those two debates, the Hartford and then San Diego, you were behind in the polls. Did you feel that, hey, this is an opportunity to turn this thing around? Did you think they were that important?"

"You feel that way, but then you've got to determine how am I going to turn it around. That's the hard part. You know, if lightning strikes and he may hit a home run somewhere, but it doesn't happen in debates. . . . We couldn't figure out any way, at least I couldn't, how . . . to open it up without getting nasty, mean, personal, whatever. And I didn't want to do that."

Would it have mattered to the final outcome if he had?

"I don't think it would have made much of a difference," Dole answered. But I detected a whiff of something in his tone and body language that added a forlorn "maybe" to his response.

There were no character questions from the citizens at the San Diego debate, of course.

Clinton assumed that would be the case. "It's a little harder in those debates to go after your opponent unless people serve you up the right question. Otherwise the picture is of a debater being disrespectful to the citizens."

He, unlike most other candidates, acknowledged that he had used some prepackaged lines, particularly when he said, "I can only tell you that I don't think Senator Dole is too old to be president. It's the age of his ideas that I question."

Said Clinton, "[About the only thing you can do is] leave a memorable line or two in the public consciences [like when] President Reagan said, 'There you go again'—that kind of thing. So . . . you try, at least I did . . . to take two or three or four of those lines in my head into all these debates, and then if I got the chance to use them, I did, and if it didn't seem appropriate, I didn't."

Jack Kemp, who, like Dole, took a pass on bringing up the Clinton character issue in his debate with Gore, had a slightly different take on what happened. He said he had misunderstood my first question and thought I was talking only about personal issues rather than ethical.

"I clearly missed the opportunity to take on the fact that President Clinton had said he was going to have the most ethical administration in the history of America, and he was vulnerable there. . . . I got heavily, heavily criticized for that, and it was probably weakness on my part."

Kemp said Gore didn't help matters.

"He played a dirty trick on me—called me a nice guy and that just totally unnerved me and ruined my political career."

That was not literally true, of course. Jack Kemp, a gregariously accessible man to journalists as well as voters, lived a life that was way beyond normal politics. He had represented Buffalo, New York, in the House of Representatives for eighteen years after doing so as a star quarterback for the Buffalo Bills in what was then the American Football League.

"Pro football gave me a good sense of perspective to enter politics," Kemp once said. "I'd already been booed, cheered, cut, sold, traded, and hung in effigy."

That quote is from a superb May 2009 *New York Times* obituary by Adam Clymer that appeared upon Kemp's death from cancer at age seventy-three.

CHAPTER 5

The Big Sighs

Newspaper city room lore says the best-ever lead sentence on a murder trial story went something like this:

"Accused mob killer Jimmy 'Potatoes' Gardner took the witness stand in his own defense today and talked himself to death."

Novelists as diverse as Kurt Vonnegut and Booth Tarkington have used that "talked himself to death" line in different contexts.

Similarly, a derivative summary of the first 2000 presidential debate could go:

"Vice President Al Gore debated Texas governor George W. Bush at the University of Massachusetts in Boston last night and sighed himself to death."

But I, the moderator, missed the sighing—as Carole Simpson had done with George H. W. Bush's watch-watching in 1992.

While walking out of the hall with family after the debate my daughter Amanda commented, in passing, about that being "really something" what Gore had done.

I didn't know what she was talking about. I had a rule about watching the candidate who was talking, never the one who was listening. I didn't want any candidate to use eye contact with me as a way to transmit his own reactions.

So, despite being the physically closest person in the room—just ten feet away from both candidates—I ended up missing what turned out to be the most important story of that debate.

Through the television device of a split screen, the world watched as Gore on that October 3 evening expressed disgust and displeasure with Bush's answers.

Gore sighed heavily and repeatedly. He shook his head, frowned, rolled his eyes, and sneered. And—one thing I did know for sure—he also violated the time limits for questions and responses, ignored the polite pleas of the moderator, and, generally, came across as overbearing—unlikable.

That, at least, was the consensus reaction from even his own supporters as well as much of the public. Gore was judged the clear loser in the debate, based almost entirely on his body language and not on what he actually said. As with the first Kennedy-Nixon debate in 1960, radio listeners came away with an entirely different impression from that of those who watched it on television.

The parallels are consistent. Gore and Bush, like Kennedy and Nixon, were running from their respective lefts and rights toward the centrist middle where general elections are won and lost. They were also carefully rounding off and away from sharp differences.

The overall theme of the Boston debate, agreed to by the candidates and the debate commission, was domestic policy. But nothing said by either Gore or Bush caused any ripples except a few lines using "fuzzy math" on taxes and "lockbox" in exchanges over Medicare and Social Security.

Based on a coin toss, the first question went to Gore.

"Vice President Gore, you have questioned whether Governor Bush has the experience to be president of the United States. What exactly do you mean?"

Gore responded by thanking the debate sponsors and the people of Boston and then said: "I have actually not questioned Governor Bush's experience. I have questioned his proposals and here is why. . . ."

He then went on for his opening two minutes to summarize his own campaign agenda.

After a back-and-forth on Gore's answer, I asked Bush what I had designed to be an apples-to-apples companion inquiry:

"You have questioned whether Vice President Gore has demonstrated the leadership qualities necessary to be president of the United States. What do you mean?"

Bush answered: "Actually, what I've said, Jim, I've said that eight years ago they campaigned on prescription drugs for seniors. And four years ago they campaigned on getting prescription drugs for seniors. And now they're campaigning on getting prescription drugs for seniors. It seems like they can't get it done."

Bush then added that it was time to get some people in Washington who would work with both Republicans and Democrats to get results when it comes to seniors.

Thus, right at the beginning, here now was the mutual no-elbows approach in action. Neither Bush nor Gore took up the invitation to go on the attack against the other's principal soft spot—at least as seen at the time by the polls and other measurements of the conventional wisdom.

That left mostly only the Big Sigh criticism in the wake of the Boston debate.

This led Gore's advisers to work on ways to repair the damage in the next two debates. As a result, Gore played quiet and nice a week later seated at a table with Bush at Wake Forest University in Winston-Salem, North Carolina.

Then, after being criticized for being too passive in Winston-Salem, he went on the offensive again in the third debate, a town hall format in St. Louis. He wore boots and a long-cut suit to make him look bigger and stronger than Bush and, in a most bizarre move, during one exchange walked right at Bush as if he were going to confront him physically.

Gore came across as three different personalities in three different debates. His chameleon-like changes were disconcerting to some voters. But the bottom line may be that Gore was already a goner in Boston before the other two debates and long before anything happened later in the precincts of Florida or at the U.S. Supreme Court. That is for historians to resolve.

The three Gore-Bush debates happened over fourteen days. The invitation to moderate all three had come early to me from the debate commission. I was told there was little consultation about my selection with the candidates' representatives.

What I know for certain is that the pace was punishing for everyone involved—including me.

THE SECOND PRESIDENTIAL debate, a sit-down event in Wake Forest University's Wait Chapel on October 11, 2000, focused on foreign policy.

Nothing occurred during those ninety minutes that would qualify as a Major Moment, either in spoken or body language. But, in light of later events, there was a most interesting pre-9/11 exchange about Iraq.

The candidates discussed how best to use the enormous power of the United States, with Gore conceding that there weren't that many differences between him and Bush.

> BUSH: That's hard to tell. I think that, you know, I would hope to be able to convince people I could handle the Iraqi situation better.
>
> LEHRER: Saddam Hussein, you mean, get him out of there?
>
> BUSH: I'd like to, of course, and I presume this administration would as well. We don't know—there are no inspectors now in Iraq, the coalition that was in place isn't as strong as it used to be. He is a danger. We don't want him fishing in troubled waters in the Middle East. And it's going to be hard, it's going to be important to rebuild that coalition to keep the pressure on him.
>
> LEHRER: You feel that is a failure of the Clinton administration?
>
> BUSH: I do.
>
> GORE: Well, when I got to be a part of the current administration, it was right after—I was one of the few members of my political party to support former presi-

dent Bush in the Persian Gulf War resolution, and at the end of that war, for whatever reason, it was not finished in a way that removed Saddam Hussein from power. I know there are all kinds of circumstances and explanations. But the fact is that that's the situation that was left when I got there. And we have maintained the sanctions. Now I want to go further. I want to give robust support to the groups that are trying to overthrow Saddam Hussein, and I know there are allegations that they're too weak to do it, but that's what they said about the forces that were opposing Milosevic in Serbia, and you know, the policy of enforcing sanctions against Serbia has just resulted in a spectacular victory for democracy just in the past week, and it seems to me that having taken so long to see the sanctions work there, building upon the policy of containment that was successful over a much longer period of time against the former Soviet Union in the Communist bloc, seems a little early to declare that we should give up on the sanctions. I know the governor's not necessarily saying that but, you know, all of these flights that have come in, all of them have been in accordance with the sanctions regime, I'm told, except for three where they notified, and they're trying to break out of the box, there's no question about it. I don't think they should be allowed to.

LEHRER: [*to Bush*] Did he state your position correctly, you're not calling for eliminating the sanctions, are you?

BUSH: No, of course not, absolutely not, I want them to be tougher.

I took the discussion on to the troubles over the breakup of Yugoslavia and whether the ouster of Milosevic as president should be seen as a triumph for U.S. military intervention.

Many words later Bush and Gore agreed—yes, it was such a triumph.

Then, at the very end before closing statements, there was a brief exchange that led to my most precarious—and hellish— few days as a debate moderator. In the language of my walking-the-knife analogy, I slipped off the blade and got cut.

I questioned Bush about post-Boston charges from his campaign that Gore "exaggerates, embellishes, and stretches the facts." I asked the governor if he saw this as a serious issue.

BUSH: Well, we all make mistakes. I've been known to mangle a syllable or two myself, you know, if you know what I mean. I think credibility is important. It is going to be important for the president to be credible with Congress, important for the president to be credible with foreign nations. And yes, I think it's something that people need to consider. This isn't something new. I read a report, or a memo, from somebody in his 1988 campaign—I forgot the fellow's name—warning then Senator Gore to be careful about exaggerating claims. . . .

I am going to continue to defend my record and defend my propositions against what I think are exaggerations. Exaggerations like, for example, only five percent of seniors receive benefits under my Medicare reform package. That's what he said the other day, and that's simply not the case. And I have every right in the world to defend my record and positions. That's what debates are about and that's what campaigns are about.

Gore admitted he got some details wrong in the Boston debate and promised to do better.

GORE: There are seniors who pay more for their prescriptions than a lot of other people, more than their pets, sometimes. More sometimes than people in foreign countries. And we need to do something about that. Not with the measure that leaves the majority of them without any real basic help until the next president's term of four years is over. But right away. And that means doing it under the Medicare program. I can't promise that I will never get another detail wrong. . . .

A moment later I asked Bush if that resolved the exaggeration issue for him.

BUSH: That's going to be up to the people, isn't it?

LEHRER: Does it resolve it for *you*?

BUSH: Depends on what he says in the future in the campaign.

LEHRER: Your folks are saying some awful things.

BUSH: I hope they're not awful things. I think they may be using the man's own words.

LEHRER: Well, what I mean is calling him a serial exaggerator—

BUSH: I don't believe I've used those words.

LEHRER: No, but they have in your campaign ads.

BUSH: Maybe they have.

Then I turned to Gore.

LEHRER: And your campaign officials have . . . *your* campaign officials, Mr. Vice President, are now calling the governor a bumbler.

BUSH: Wait a minute.

LEHRER: I mean, my point is, should this—is this—

GORE: I don't use language like that and I don't think that we should.

LEHRER: It's in your commercial.

GORE: I understand. The—I haven't seen that, in my commercials?

BUSH: You haven't seen the commercial?

LEHRER: Your—

GORE: I think that what—I think the point of that is that anybody would have a hard time trying to make a tax cut plan that is so large, that would put us into such big deficits, that gives almost half the benefits to the wealthiest of the wealthy. I think anybody would have a hard time explaining that clearly in a way that makes sense to the average person.

BUSH: That's the kind of exaggeration I was just talking about.

GORE: Well, I wasn't the one having trouble explaining it.

"IT'S IN YOUR commercial."

That line stuck with me like tar from Winston-Salem to St. Louis, site of the next debate, and through Gore campaign operatives to *The New York Times*.

First, a Gore representative complained through *NewsHour* executive producer Les Crystal, claiming that no Gore commercial ever made the charge that Bush was a bumbler. It was a campaign spokesman who said it.

The Gore complainant also itemized other alleged mistakes I had made in the first two debates.

The next thing I knew, a political reporter for the *Times* was calling me for comment—for my reaction to several complaints about my moderating, including the ones from the Gore people.

The resulting story appeared under the headline THE 2000 CAMPAIGN: THE DEBATES; CRITICS ACCUSE MODERATOR OF LETTING DEBATE WANDER.

The text concentrated on my not being aggressive enough, not "accentuating the differences" in my questions. A former Democratic presidential adviser accused me of not pressing the candidates and, most colorfully, "running the debates as though they were some kind of sherry hour at the institute of politics at Harvard."

The jab that mattered the most to me, however, came from Bob Kerrey, then a Democratic senator and Gore surrogate, who said: "You could have picked 10 people off the street who didn't know Jerusalem from Georgia and they would have had better questions."

I had known and interviewed Kerrey many times, going back to his pre-politics days in Nebraska as an angry Vietnam War veteran.

After the *Times* story ran, Kerrey left a recorded message on my home phone in Washington apologizing for what he said, claiming he didn't really mean it and spoke only because "Rick Berke [the *Times* reporter] called me and said he needed a 'hot quote knocking Lehrer' for his story."

I don't know the truth of Kerrey's claim because I have never taken the time to run it down. But I have no doubt that the same Gore campaign operatives who successfully pushed Berke to do the story also suggested Kerrey be interviewed.

There were other critics of those 2000 debates. National newspaper columnists as varied politically as Bob Herbert and William Safire of *The New York Times* and Richard Cohen of *The Washington Post* also took pokes at me. The cheapest of the shots was a one-liner in *Time* magazine, made cheaper because it was anonymously fired.

It is possible that every word of criticism, including Kerrey's, was spoken honestly—and was justified. I didn't think so at the time and, mostly, I still don't. But so what?

Such stories, of course, are more likely to be pursued and printed than all others—particularly in the field of political journalism, where the rules for using anonymous sources range from loose to nonexistent.

What the *Times* and others did was confirm what my family and friends already knew: I do not handle criticism well.

Bottom line, the Gore people eventually got some of what they wanted. But not before I spent a full day in real hell.

———

THAT POST-WINSTON-SALEM *New York Times* story came out the day of the third presidential debate at Washington University in St. Louis. I had spent time—too much, in retrospect—dealing with it in the days before, counseling with *NewsHour* folks, talking to the reporter, anguishing with Kate and our daughter Jamie, who was with us in St. Louis.

But much more important on the hell scale for me, the commission and candidates had agreed on a town hall process that was drastically different from the 1996 event in San Diego.

This time, the moderator would be in charge of it all.

I would be given the questions in advance and select which ones to use. I would then brief representatives of the candidates on the method I used for selecting "the questions at random while assuring that questions are reasonably well balanced in terms of addressing a wide range of issues of major public interest facing the United States and the world," according to the rules agreed to by each candidate.

I met with the 140 citizen-questioners, gave them a briefing and preaching similar to the one in San Diego, and asked, finally, that each write two questions on separate pieces of paper and make an extra copy for me—and only me.

That whole process took more than two hours.

After that, I went to the briefing of the candidates' people. Janet Brown of the commission was also present for the meeting at the office of the Washington University athletic director, where I was working. That lasted another thirty minutes. I talked only process, of course—not the content of the questions.

I looked at a wall clock. I could not believe that I suddenly had so little time left to sort through nearly three hundred questions, each on a small piece of paper. Kate and Jamie joined *NewsHour* staffers Les Crystal and Annette Miller in frantically separating them in stacks by subject and then by quality.

As in San Diego, I knew that only about twenty would actually be heard by anyone in the debate itself.

A moment was rapidly approaching when I honestly believed we might not make it in time. I was going to have to look out at a television camera and say something like:

"Good evening from the Field House at Washington University in St. Louis. I'm Jim Lehrer of *The NewsHour* on PBS and I'm sorry to report that I am not quite ready for tonight's presidential debate between Vice President Al Gore and Governor George W. Bush. So we're going to play music—something from Mozart or the Beatles, possibly, or feel free to talk among yourselves while you wait."

The last critical task, which Kate and I did literally with only a few minutes to go, was check the chosen few for a balanced race, gender, and age mix. PC or not, that had to be done. I felt strongly that the very nature of this event demanded that the diversity of the American electorate's representatives be recognizable beyond just their questions.

I went out to the hall, did my introductions and cautions to the audience, and prepared to go on the air. I took my seat and got hooked up, as always, to two microphones in case one went bad and to an earpiece so I could hear cues from the debate executive producer.

After several sound checks, I arranged my papers on the

small table before me and took one of the longest breaths of my life.

Suddenly there was no noise in my ear. A crew member on-stage told me that the debate executive producer, Marty Slutsky, was saying things to me. (Slutsky had replaced Ed Fouhy in that job by then.)

I could not hear Slutsky.

"Lost audio!" I said firmly, barely able to keep sheer panic out of my voice. Everyone in the hall, including both Mrs. Bush and Mrs. Gore and their families, went absolutely silent. Everyone could tell I was in trouble.

"Working on audio!" someone on the crew announced loudly to all. "Three minutes to air!"

"It's okay with me if you don't take the full three minutes to fix it," I said with a false tone of confidence and coolness. This was pressure beyond most anything I had even imagined before.

There was a sympathetic round of laughs and small applause for me in the hall, which I appreciated.

The only serious audio problem I had dealt with previously was during the October 11, 1992, Bush-Clinton-Perot debate, also at Washington University in St. Louis. During that entire ninety minutes, someone backstage had inadvertently left open his internal communications mike in the control room. As a result, I had the distraction of hearing every behind-the-scenes word spoken to him and by him. The fact that I did not miss any cues or many words spoken by the candidates was a miracle.

Now, eight years later, I was really proud of myself for fighting my natural instinct to scream something profane that would not only be heard in the hall but by viewers of C-SPAN, which was broadcasting the pre-debate activities.

Then, with less than thirty seconds to go, I heard the magic words, "Jim! Jim! Can you hear me now?"

I could.

I did my welcome, explained the rules, and announced to the television world:

"Before we begin, a correction from last week's debate. I was wrong when I said Vice President Gore's campaign commercials had called Governor Bush a bumbler. That specific charge was made in a press statement by Gore campaign spokesman Mark Fabiani, not in a TV commercial."

Gore said to me: "I'm glad you clarified that."

The studio audience, possibly puzzled along with the rest of America about the real difference between a commercial and a press statement, laughed uncomfortably.

I then called on the first citizen questioner—a man concerned about HMOs and insurance companies—instead of medical professionals—making decisions that affect people's lives.

But the trip to hell and beyond was not quite over.

About two-thirds of the way through the ninety minutes and fifteen questions, Gore began his menacing march across the stage directly toward Bush. I thought, Oh, my God! Gore's going to physically attack Bush! Do a body block, a head butt—something.

I had tried to imagine every calamity that could possibly happen in any given debate. I had, indeed, silently rehearsed to myself what I would say if any candidate continually refused to obey the time-limit rules, as I thought Dole might do in a Hail Mary attempt at that critical 1996 Hartford debate with Clinton.

But I was not prepared for leaping, boxing-referee fashion, into a physical fray between two candidates.

Fortunately, Bush merely gave the approaching Gore a puzzled smile, stepped to one side, and continued saying whatever he was saying in response to an audience question about voter apathy.

And my trip to hell ended—finally.

MY OPPORTUNITY TO get George W. Bush's debate reflections came on January 16, 2007, after a twenty-five-minute *NewsHour* interview in the White House Cabinet Room. The premise was a State of the Union preview, and much of the time was devoted to the Iraq war.

The debates came up in the pre-interview chat, while our technicians were testing camera shots and sound.

Bush, in a good humor, asked me: "You think they'll recycle you for one more election cycle?"

I said probably not—no thanks. I've done enough of them already, and I've got the scars on my psyche to prove it. I then quickly put in a pitch to interview him sometime for an update of our earlier debates documentary.

"Well, why don't we do it at the end of this?" he said.

I was not really prepared, but I said, Yes, sir, fine with me. A bird in the hand in the presidential interview business is . . . well, a Bush in the hand.

So after I said, "Thank you, Mr. President," to end the main interview, a new tape was inserted in our cameras and we started talking about debates.

Bush had been understandably tight and careful during the previous twenty-five minutes, but now he was relaxed and grinning.

As for Gore's sighing in the first debate in Boston, Bush had an experience similar to mine.

"I didn't have any idea it was going on. I really didn't. I was so focused that when it was over, somebody, I can't remember who it was, Karen [Hughes] or Karl Rove or somebody, said, you are not going to believe Al Gore's facial expressions. Really cost him the debate, they thought."

It was in the third debate, of course, when Gore's aggression reached its Major Moment pinnacle during an exchange about HMOs, health insurance companies, and a patients' bill of rights.

Bush's version:

"I was prowling a little bit, but so was Gore. And he approached me at first and I wasn't certain what was happening, and it looked like it was going to be the body bump—the chest bump. I think, as I recall, I gave him an odd-expression kind of a look. I couldn't tell if he was trying to threaten me, in which case it amused me even more or—I wasn't sure what his motives were. All I can tell you is that, I think if you review the tape you will see a bemused expression on my face.

"The other option would have been to go for the huge chest bump, which in itself maybe decided the debate, and he was bigger than I am. . . ."

———

I REGRET THAT I was never able to secure an interview with Gore about any of his debates, the three in 2000 as well as the 1992 vice presidential debate, and even the NAFTA event with Ross Perot. A sweep through the press coverage of the 2000 debates produced only a few Gore comments.

I have only one statement to report on my own.

He said it to me as the Gore and Bush families and major supporters exchanged greetings on the St. Louis stage at the end of that third and final debate. Photos were being taken with some of the members of the questioning audience, part of a process that is no longer permitted, presumably, for security reasons.

Gore, in a reference to the Goldilocks fairy tale, said to me, "In the first debate I was too hot, in the second I was too cold, and in the third I was just right."

He repeated that take in a 2002 CNN interview with Paula Zahn, saying that he and his wife, Tipper, had said that to each other right after the debates ended.

Zahn asked Gore if he felt manipulated by his handlers—if they had tried to make him be someone he wasn't.

"No," said Gore. "If I had any criticism, it would be of myself for, you know, not just focusing on the things that mattered the most."

He said that immediately after the first debate his advisers got him to watch a *Saturday Night Live* satire of what he had done. "'Hey, look, during those cutaways, the reaction shots, you know, the sighing stuff.' It made it easier for me to see what didn't—what wasn't good about that, sure."

I have no trouble understanding why Al Gore has not talked at length about the 2000 debates—with me or anyone else. He has had little to say about that entire election process, which resulted in the most agonizing finish ever for a presidential candidate. Despite the wounds from that experience, some of which may never fully heal, he has moved on to an honored place as a world advocate for environmental causes.

My guess is that someday he will tell his story of 2000 in a well-written book that will, in fact, include specifics about how he was hurt by some of his campaign friends as much as by his enemies—and his sighing.

FOR SOMETHING ENTIRELY different. . . .

There was the vice presidential debate of former defense secretary and Republican congressman Dick Cheney of Wyoming and Democratic senator Joe Lieberman of Connecticut.

The candidates met on October 5, 2000—between the first and second Gore-Bush debates—at the campus of Centre College in Danville, Kentucky. CNN's Bernard Shaw moderated.

Lieberman told me in our documentary interview that about a week or ten days before the debate Gore called him and said, "'Are you getting ready for the debate?' I said, 'Yes, I am.' He said, 'You know what Cheney is going to do during the whole debate, don't you?' I said, 'What?' He said, 'He's going to attack me. So your job is to defend me.'"

Lieberman said Gore told him that he based that on his own '92 vice presidential debate experience with Dan Quayle and James Stockdale, when Quayle spent the whole night attacking Clinton.

On the other hand, Cheney said in his documentary chat that after watching tapes of Lieberman's Senate campaign debates in Connecticut, particularly against Republican Lowell Weicker, he, too, was expecting a rough time.

"Joe was very tough. Those debates with Weicker were a knock-down, drag-out kind of an affair. So I went in prepared for that possibility."

But there were no knockdowns, no tough talk—or even any Major Moments.

Cheney concluded that the format, first suggested by the debate commission, contributed to the tone.

"I am a great believer that the physical arrangements are important, and the one condition that we had both in 2000 and in 2004 in terms of the negotiations prior to the debate was that I wanted to be seated at a table. I wanted the format like this or as on *Meet the Press* or your show on PBS. The bit with the podium and the staging and the certain spacing between the podiums—those kind of arrangements always gave it a sort of stilted affair, and I was much more comfortable sitting down and talking. And both times we were successful. We had that as our sort of nonnegotiable demand for the vice presidential debate, and both times they agreed."

I asked Lieberman if he was aware of any of that.

"It's interesting. Nobody's told me that before. . . . There was a team negotiating, and they came back to me and said we are going to do this seated, and I must admit my first response was 'Gee, that's strange. I've done all my other debates, Senate debates, standing.' And they said no, we think this will be great for you because it will make you comfortable and it will make you feel just like it is a TV interview, perhaps on the Jim Lehrer *NewsHour* or something weird like that. So that was about it."

Both candidates, in their separate interviews with me, agreed their debate was the most civilized anyone could remember. Cheney and Lieberman even assessed the debate result the same way—almost.

Cheney said he definitely believed he won it.

Lieberman said, "I'll tell you something, I think both Dick Cheney and I did well in that debate, and I suppose I would say both of us gained and therefore maybe both of us were winners."

Bernard Shaw told me:

"It was fascinating sitting there. They were real statesmen debating. I think the format had everything to do with it. Apart from the qualities of these two public servants, they were seated almost elbow to elbow. It's hard to batter a guy sitting next to you. You have to really look him in the eye and address the issue on the table."

Shaw added that a lot of people after the debate "said both parties should have flipped their tickets and put Lieberman at the top for the Democrats and Cheney at the top for the Republicans."

That thought should serve as a mind-rattling reminder of how things can shift in the world of American politics.

Lieberman was defeated in 2006 for the Democratic renomination to the U.S. Senate from Connecticut mostly because of his support for the U.S.-led war in Iraq. But he won reelection as an independent and went on to endorse Republican John McCain against Democrat Barack Obama for president in 2010.

CHAPTER 6

Play-by-Plays

Then came the Year of Our Politics 2004 when I moderated the first debate between President George W. Bush and Senator John Kerry.

A personal play-by-play:

The official call came from Janet Brown, with whom I had become foxhole comrades after sharing the experiences of nine previous debates. Brown was the first and the only executive director of the Commission on Presidential Debates there has ever been. She is, without any doubt, the central driving force behind the commission's life and work.

By the time of her call, the commission had already announced the 2004 dates, places, and formats of three presidential and one vice presidential debate.

"I hereby ask if you would moderate the first presidential debate between President Bush and Senator Kerry on September 30, 2004," Brown said with an embellished tone of phony formality. "The subject will be domestic policy; the location will be the University of Miami at Coral Gables."

No way! That was the answer that flashed immediately in

my mind. I had already talked through such a possibility with Kate. Nine debates were enough. The stress and strain of 2000 had left me determined to rest forever on my arrows and/or laurels.

I felt I had done my duty for my country and, yes, my ego. I had, in fact, proclaimed to Brown quite forcefully, "This is *it* for me!" during a debriefing session a few weeks after the 2000 debates.

Now, four years later, I told Brown that I was honored to be asked again, but my inclination remained to take a pass on doing it one more time. But give me a day to talk to Kate and the girls—daughters Jamie, Lucy, and Amanda—before giving a final answer.

The family consensus was easily reached. Do what *you* want to do. But that was accompanied by strong reminders about the various hells of 2000, and the potential for it happening again. There also was stern unanimity for absolutely refusing to do more than one debate this time, no matter what.

I called Brown the next day and accepted the invitation to moderate the Bush-Kerry debate in Florida on September 30.

CBS's Bob Schieffer and Charles Gibson of ABC agreed to moderate the other two Bush-Kerry presidential debates, and my *NewsHour* colleague Gwen Ifill did the same for the vice presidential conversation between Vice President Cheney and Senator John Edwards.

The debate commission had taken a major step toward declaring its independence. The moderator selections and the location decisions had not been run by Kerry and Bush representatives in advance, much less negotiated with them officially.

Since some of the Kerry consultants were Gore leftovers with 2000 grievances, I heard there were internal grumblings, particularly about my selection as a moderator.

There had also been some indications that the Bush campaign was interested in fewer debates this time and in using other sponsors besides the commission. The networks, most particularly NBC and some of the cables, were reported to be hustling behind the scenes to stage their own debates.

Heavy guns were brought in. Former secretary of state James Baker was named to head a committee to negotiate for Bush. Lawyer, investment banker, and Clinton friend Vernon Jordan would do the same for Kerry, who immediately agreed to the commission's plan. Bush did not.

There were negotiations about the negotiations, and finally a thirty-two-page agreement between the two candidates emerged that went into minute detail about the debates—the room temperature, the use of notes at podiums, even the size of the various holding rooms at the debate sites.

The provision that drew the most attention, however, was this:

"When a candidate is speaking, either in answering a question or making his closing statement, TV coverage will be limited to the candidate speaking. There will be no TV cutaways to any candidate who is not responding to a question while another candidate is answering a question or to a candidate who is not giving a closing statement while another candidate is doing so."

That was clearly aimed at avoiding a repeat of anything resembling Gore-like Big Sigh shots.

The rules on timing and length of answers and responses were also strict, designed to discourage either candidate from going beyond the short and the well-rehearsed. Avoiding mistakes had definitely returned as the principal mission.

There were open spaces, properly labeled, at the end of the written document for signatures by commission members and the four moderators. There was a strong suggestion leaked in the press that there might not be any debates at all if the commission members didn't sign.

And any moderator who didn't sign might be replaced.

Not even negotiating committees run by James Baker and Vernon Jordan could have lived with the repercussions from that nonsense.

By now any threat—real or implied—to refuse to debate was as empty as it was ridiculous. And everybody knew it. The debate imperative was firmly established.

Neither the commission members nor any of the moderators signed anything. The commission agreed to the basic questioning rules but took the position that it did not have the power to dictate where and how the network pool cameras would cover the debates.

We moderators simply reaffirmed—by phone to Janet Brown—that we accepted the invitation. Each of us made it clear that we would neither sign nor make any other arrangement with the candidates.

I began diving into the mountains of Bush-Kerry research the *NewsHour* staff had prepared for me on domestic issues. . . .

Then came another call from Janet Brown. The commission had agreed to a candidates' request that the subjects of the first and second debates be switched. Instead of domestic, the first one would now be foreign affairs and homeland security; the second would focus on domestic issues.

"Let's just trade debates," said Schieffer, an old friend, in a separate call to me minutes later. He was by then as deep in foreign affairs/security as I was in domestic. But trading debates at this late date was not an option, we were quickly told by the commission. The order of the debates and the moderators had been agreed upon. Don't rock the boat.

So at Bob's suggestion, he and I simply exchanged questions. I sent over all of my domestic research to Schieffer at his office at the CBS News Washington bureau, and he forwarded his foreign material to me. (Neither of us, it turned out, used the other's questions word for word, but they were of great help to both of us.)

Then on September 20, 2004, ten days before the first debate was scheduled, Baker and Jordan put out an eleven-sentence joint statement:

"We are pleased to announce today that President Bush and Senator Kerry will participate in three debates." That was the first sentence. "We wish to commend the Commission on Presidential Debates for its efforts on the 2004 debates," was number eleven.

Those in between simply repeated what the commission had announced earlier, including the moderators. The only major change had been the domestic/foreign–national security switch between the first and second debates. Otherwise, the commission's unilateral decisions on the basics stood—and, with it, increased independence.

Beyond the basic research, the big issue confronting me was how to deal with the actual rules of the debate. The commission had conceded a return to limits that specifically precluded direct exchanges between candidates and, in my opinion, discouraged follow-ups and free-flowing discussion.

I spent considerable time figuring out ways I might be able to make it work better without violating the letter of the rules or my promise to implement them.

There were two categories of questions: response and new question. I made a series of elaborate charts for tracking how I would go from one to the other in such a way that might create a flow.

And, behind a closed door in my Washington office, I practiced using those charts. I considered a few likely answers from Bush and Kerry and worked through several possibilities of what I could do if one said this, the other said that—back and forth, on and on. It took many hours and much concentration but it did finally result in my going into a comfort zone much sooner than I had expected.

I even had a couple of mornings when I didn't wake up wide-eyed with the frantic thought *Oh, my God! Is this the day of the debate?* That had been part of my anxiety pattern going back to that first 1988 Dukakis-Bush debate.

The zone held as Kate and I went off to Miami, along with what I called our "moderator fire team." They were *NewsHour* executive producer Les Crystal, a man of grace and experience who made sure every production base was covered on my behalf. Annette Miller, head of our research operation, created an editorial room for any late-breaking news or information I needed to absorb. Tim Perry, our tech expert extraordinaire, set up computers and printers. Marge Hubbard, the queen of makeup, was there to cover up the huge bags that have been under my eyes since hours after I was born.

We were met at the Miami airport by Carlene Ackerman, a commission volunteer who drew the daunting assignment of "seeing to" all moderator wants and needs, as she had in 2000 and would do again in 2008. Ackerman once worked as executive assistant to then secretary of state Warren Christopher. She was—is—the best.

The headquarters hotel was the Biltmore in Coral Gables, which billed itself as "A Culmination of Exceptional Grace, Style and Beauty."

Soon Jamie, Lucy, and Amanda arrived, along with other members of our family. I had invited everyone to come on the grounds that this would definitely be the last one of "these things" I would ever do.

Among the major attractions for the kids was a white stretch limousine that was provided to take us where we needed to go.

On debate morning, one of those trips was to a men's clothing store in Coral Gables for me to buy a new tie to wear at the debate. That custom began when Lucy and Amanda went with Crystal, Miller, and me to buy a tie the afternoon of the 1996 Clinton-Dole debate in Hartford.

Bush-Kerry was a bright red thing that cost $145.

The distance from the hotel to the debate site, the University of Miami Convocation Center, was short—thank God. There were fourteen of us from the family and team crammed into the back of the limo, high school prom–style.

There were no security hassles this time. The only critical moment came when our eighteen-month-old granddaughter Olivia had her diaper-covered bottom checked by a Secret Service agent with a handheld metal detector. We assumed the agent was a man with a sense of humor.

We were installed in the office of the University of Miami women's basketball coach. It included plenty of space for the entourage as well as a desk with a computer and printer that Perry had set up for me.

That first debate experience Kate and I shared at Winston-Salem in 1988 alerted us to the obvious fact that precise knowledge is everything in a debate operation.

Standard candidate preparation includes mock debate sessions with questions campaign advisers deem the most likely to be asked. Such advisers are known for their intensity in scooping up every scintilla of information that could be helpful.

Kerry did his pre-Miami prep at a resort in Wisconsin. Former Clinton White House lawyer Greg Craig played Bush. Bob Shrum, a Democratic consultant who had worked in the Gore campaign, was the stand-in moderator. New Hampshire senator Judd Gregg played Kerry at Bush's Texas ranch rehearsals. Republican media consultant Mark McKinnon starred as the moderator. Gregg had also played Gore for the 2000 Bush mock-ups, and Craig had been Bush for Gore. Maybe the similarity in names leads to fitness for playing presidential candidates in mock debates?

Whatever, five days before the Miami debate, while still in Washington, I had ceased discussing what I might ask either Bush or Kerry, including with members of our own *NewsHour* staff. I did not want anyone to be put in the position of having to lie about what they might know of what was to come.

I also never ever let the loose-leaf binder with my question work notes out of my own hands. I didn't actually put them under the pillow, but it was close.

Two hours before the debate, I went into a private room with Kate—and only Kate—and ran through my debate strategy and read the probable questions out loud. That final check with Kate had been a ritual ever since Winston-Salem, even when we had to do it by phone.

As always, Kate had reactions—and suggestions.

And, as always, I took every one of them. . . .

Twenty minutes before 9 p.m. eastern time, I was escorted out of the coach's office to the stage.

One of the rules that the commission adopted after 1992 was strict silence from the audience in the hall. So after being introduced to the audience of six hundred people chosen by the campaigns and debate sponsors, I laid down the law. I reminded everyone that they were not there to participate. This was not a talent show. Applause, cheers, hisses, and/or boos to demonstrate approval or disapproval were not only not permitted; they were mortal sins. I told them that if this rule was ever violated, I would stop the debate, turn around, and point to the culprit before a national television audience that would most likely include everyone they have ever known in their lives.

I said it all with a smile, but I meant every word.

Then I took my seat at the moderating desk, with my back to the audience, and got ready for what was to come.

One of the reasons I was at a comfort level that let me

proceed without breaking into hives or the shakes was the commission's production and technical staff. My confidence in them, as usual, gave me some of my own.

Executive producer Marty Slutsky is not only a longtime network producer; he's also an accomplished guitarist, his major gig having been with the well-known folk-rock band McKendree Spring. Larry Estrin led the audio crew, who with Russell Emery, were the heroes in 2000 who got sound back in my ear in St. Louis. Paul Byers was the timer in charge of the clock and colored lights. John Hodges, Michael Foley, and several others on the production crew designed and constructed the sets.

Slutsky in his quiet voice, counted me down and cued me.

"Good evening from the University of Miami Convocation Center in Coral Gables, Florida."

The TelePrompTer was working and visible through a slit in the TV-set background. No problem. I went through the basics, pointing out that while the umbrella topic was foreign policy and homeland security, the specific areas were chosen by me, as were the questions. The candidates did not know what the questions would be.

"For each question there can only be a two-minute response, a ninety-second rebuttal, and, at my discretion, a discussion extension of one minute."

I reminded everyone that, under the rules, the candidates could not direct questions to each other. And I went through the green, yellow, and red light system for timing answers and the fact that now there was even a "backup buzzer system if needed." That also, I assumed, was a residue of Gore and 2000. If a candidate went over a particular time limit and the moderator was unable to shut him up, then, via the loud sound of the buzzer, everyone on the planet would know. It reminded me of the technique developed years ago to signal grade-schoolers that recess was over.

President Bush and Senator Kerry were introduced, and they took their positions at their respective podiums.

"As determined by a coin toss, the first question goes to you, Senator Kerry. You have two minutes.

"Do you believe you could do a better job than President Bush in preventing another 9/11-type terrorist attack on the United States?"

And we were off.

"Yes, I do," Kerry replied immediately, and then after some mandatory words about the debate hosts added, among other things, "I can make America safer than President Bush had made us."

Bush, in his rebuttal, did not respond directly. Under the rules, the next two-minute question went to him.

"Do you believe the election of Senator Kerry on November the second would increase the chances of the U.S. being hit by another 9/11-type attack?"

I was a happy moderator. From my perspective, I had managed to match an apple with an apple and, in the process, also ask a follow-up!

But moments later I had a mind freeze. Kerry was speaking, but suddenly I could not remember if it was his response or the answer to a new question. My little charts were *too* elaborate. I had used check marks on them as each one-two-three grouping of questions was accomplished.

There was a check mark after "response," all right, but was it meant to be? Or did I put it there too early?

I said a quiet plea to myself and simply guessed—it was his Response. That turned out to be correct. On to Bush for a New Question!

And, for me, on to an escape from what would have been an embarrassing moment similar to when I mistakenly called a time limit on George H. W. Bush in 1988. I could do without another one of those, thank you.

I shoved the charts out of the way, never to be looked at again, and got on with it.

In a ninety-second Response, Kerry accused Bush of diverting attention and resources to invading Iraq before finishing the main post-9/11 mission against Afghanistan and Osama bin Laden.

"This president has made, I regret to say, a colossal error of judgment. And judgment is what we look for in the president of the United States of America."

Coming next, under the rules, was to be another New Question to Kerry.

"New question, two minutes, Senator Kerry. 'Colossal misjudgments.' What colossal misjudgments, in your opinion, has the president made in these areas?"

Now here was a *real* follow-up, asked within the New Question rules. It seems like a very small-potato accomplishment now, but at the time, it was a big deal—to me, at least.

And I continued to do that throughout the debate.

The next New Question, for instance, went to Bush.

"What about Senator Kerry's point, the comparison he drew between the priorities of going after Osama bin Laden and going after Saddam Hussein?"

Later, I returned to where I had begun in a New Question for Kerry.

"As president, what would you do, *specifically*, in addition to or differently, to increase the homeland security of the United States than what President Bush is doing?"

I'll admit that it was not terribly well worded, but at least my mind was unfrozen and I was keeping the flow going, using very few prepared questions. I was reacting to what had been said, the way it ought to be.

Confident now that I could make this work, I went on with questions about how to decide when to bring the troops home from Iraq, the weapons of mass destruction issue, Vietnam-Iraq comparisons, Iraq miscalculations and alleged misinformation, preemptive wars, nuclear threats from Iran and North Korea, and sending troops to stop the killing in Darfur.

One of the most telling exchanges, to me at least, came near the end when I asked Bush if there were character differences between the two serious enough to deny Kerry the presidency.

After some nice words about Kerry and his family and a joke related to both having gone to Yale, Bush accused Kerry of changing his positions on Iraq.

"You cannot lead if you send mixed messages. Mixed messages send the wrong signals to our troops. Mixed messages send the wrong signals to our allies. Mixed messages send the wrong signals to the Iraqi citizens. And that's my biggest concern about my opponent. I admire his service. But I just know how this world works, and that in the councils of government, there must be certainty from the U.S. president."

Kerry responded with praise for the Bush family as well, particularly First Lady Laura Bush, and said he was not going to talk about differences in character on grounds that it was not his job or his business. But he didn't stop there.

"But this issue of certainty. It's one thing to be certain, but you can be certain and be wrong.

"It's another to be certain and be right, or to be certain and moving in the right direction, or be certain about a principle and then learn new facts and take those new facts and put them to use in order to change and get your policy right.

"What I worry about with the president is that he's not acknowledging what's on the ground, he's not acknowledging the realities of North Korea, he's not acknowledging the truth of the science of stem-cell research or of global warming and other issues.

"And certainty sometimes can get you in trouble."

Both Bush and Kerry then agreed that nuclear proliferation was one of the most serious problems facing the security of the United States. There followed a brief back-and-forth about Russia, before the debate ended with matching two-minute closing statements.

Throughout, the candidates obeyed the time rules, for the most part. The sound of a playground buzzer was never heard. There were a few occasions, in fact, when Bush didn't use the full time he was allotted for a particular question or response. That was a debate first, at least in my experience.

The post-debate reaction, interestingly enough in light of Al Gore's Big Sighs of 2000, focused on the demeanor of President Bush. He was judged by many—and later he acknowledged it himself—as having come across as annoyed, irritated, impatient. He was even seen doing things close to Gore-like sighing.

This time I did not completely miss it, because Bush's body language, including his facial gestures, were obvious while he was answering questions as well as when he was listening to Kerry's.

Asked afterward about this, President Bush said, "I guess I didn't learn any lessons from the first debate in 2000."

"I certainly was aware of his answers and some of the body language," said Senator Kerry, "but you can never tell what is translating into that now plasma screen or box or whatever."

There was also a lingering *non*story about the so-called mystery bulge. Somebody spotted what appeared to be a small box-shaped rectangular bulge under the back of Bush's suit coat.

There was speculation that it was an electronic receiver of some kind hidden there to help prompt Bush with his answers. Or maybe it was a bulletproof vest.

No, no, said Bush spokesmen, it was the result of bad tailoring. There was nothing there but a natural "pucker." President Bush, two weeks after the debate, made light of it himself on *Good Morning America*. "I guess the assumption is that if I were straying off course they would, kind of like a hunting dog, they would punch a buzzer and I would jerk back into place. It's just absurd."

Still, the story stayed alive for several weeks on the Internet and elsewhere and, before it was over, a veteran photo-imaging specialist at NASA was recruited to do some serious inquiry.

It should come as no surprise that I, again the outsider closest to the candidates during the debate, saw no bulge. I was focused on the fronts of the president and the senator, not their backs.

There was a personal high point conclusion to that September 30, 2004, debate evening when the family and team gathered in a private dining room at the Biltmore to celebrate the thirteenth birthday of our grandson Ian.

My birthday present to Ian was my $145 red debate tie, which I took from around my neck and presented to him in the company of great cheers and fanfare.

CHARLES GIBSON OF ABC moderated the Bush-Kerry town hall debate at Washington University in St. Louis a week later. There was a moderator-in-charge process that was similar to the one in 2000, but Gibson had a much better time of it than I did.

"The fact that they allowed me to make up the rules and then to pick out the questions was really empowering," he said afterward. "I thought that in the end the public was pretty well served by the evening."

On October 13, 2004, in Tempe, Arizona, Bob Schieffer of CBS moderated the third and final Bush-Kerry event, which, after the early switch, was about domestic policy.

The major news came after Schieffer asked Kerry if he believed homosexuality was a choice. "We're all God's children, Bob. And I think if you were to talk to Dick Cheney's daughter, who is a lesbian, she would tell you that she's being who she was, she's being who she was born as. I think if you talk to anybody, it's not a choice."

That answer drew harsh criticism from Dick Cheney, among others, for bringing a personal family matter into the national political dialogue.

Did Kerry have any regrets for what he did? "No, none whatsoever. I thought the criticism was contrived and inappropriate. I was trying to show that people can be completely embracing and affectionate of it and totally accepting of it, and obviously it is also important because there's such a contradiction in the public position of that administration. So they can do it privately, but they can't do it publicly and they play to different politics, and I thought it was important for people to understand that."

Kerry and Bush understandably had many differing views of the debates, including the town hall format. Bush told me he had grown to like "moving around—it relaxes the debater."

Kerry very much disliked the format.

"I had ninety seconds to talk to America about why I thought what I thought." He cited the question about how he would rate himself as an environmentalist.

"My God, we're talking about global climate change, cancer, health, security, energy independence, pollution of our waterways, loss of our fisheries, countless issues, and we had ninety seconds to talk about it in the most viewed moment of a presidential race."

Kerry blamed all of the restrictive debate rules on Bush and his people, particularly when they insisted the answers be short and that there be no direct questions between the candidates.

The differing comments that mattered most, of course, were about substance.

I asked Bush—in the debate—if the Iraq experience made it more likely or less likely that he would take the United States into another preemptive military action.

BUSH: I would hope I never have to. I understand how hard it is to commit troops. Never wanted to commit troops. When I was running—when we had the debate in 2000, never dreamt I'd be doing that. But the enemy attacked us, Jim, and I have a solemn duty to protect the American people, to do everything I can to protect us. . . .

KERRY: Jim, the president just said something extraordinarily revealing and frankly very important in this debate. In answer to your question about Iraq and sending people into Iraq, he just said, 'The enemy attacked us.' Saddam Hussein didn't attack us. Osama bin Laden attacked us. Al Qaida attacked us. . . . That's the enemy that attacked us. That's the enemy that attacked us. That's the enemy that was allowed to walk out of those mountains. That's the enemy that is now in sixty countries, with stronger recruits. . . .

BUSH: First of all, of course I know Osama bin Laden attacked us. I know that. And secondly, to think that another round of resolutions would have caused Saddam

Hussein to disarm, disclose, is ludicrous, in my judgment.
It just shows a significant difference of opinion.

In our interview later, Kerry said he felt he had won that first debate on substance.

"I think I had an opportunity to break down the stereotypes, and I also had an opportunity to show the upside of what I was thinking and the downside of what he was thinking."

Bush conceded that he came in second in that debate, because of his facial expressions, if nothing else.

"Look, the interesting thing about presidential debates is that I don't think you ever win them, but you darn sure can lose them."

WHATEVER THE LEVEL of hostility between Kerry and Bush, the real antagonism was between their running mates.

The sit-at-a-table format did not have the calming effect for Dick Cheney and John Edwards that it did for Cheney and Joe Lieberman four years earlier.

"I didn't have those same feelings with respect to Senator Edwards," Cheney said in our documentary interview. "That was more confrontational."

Edwards agreed. "It was tense and confrontational from the beginning until the end. It was exhausting, actually, because of that."

Gwen Ifill moderated that ninety minutes at Case Western Reserve University in Cleveland.

Did Edwards go into that debate in an attack mode?

"Yeah," Edwards said afterward. "I felt that because I had watched the Cheney-Lieberman [debate] from 2000 I felt like that had gone too easy for Cheney, and I thought he needed to be challenged from the beginning so that there was a real interaction."

The debate confrontation went immediately to the Iraq war. Cheney was strongly supportive. "What we did in Iraq was exactly the right thing to do. If I had it to recommend all over again, I would recommend exactly the same course of action. The world is far safer today because Saddam Hussein is in jail, his government is no longer in power. And we did exactly the right thing."

Edwards came back. "Mr. Vice President, you are still not being straight with the American people. I mean, the reality you and George Bush continue to tell people, first, that things are going well in Iraq—the American people don't need us to explain this to them, they see it on their television every single day."

It went to Iraq and 9/11.

EDWARDS: And these connections—I want the American people to hear this very clearly. Listen carefully to what the vice president is saying, because there is no connection between Saddam Hussein and the attacks of September eleventh—period.

CHENEY: The senator has got his facts wrong. I have not suggested there's a connection between Iraq and 9/11, but there's clearly an established Iraqi track record with terror. Now, the fact of the matter is, the big difference here, Gwen, is they [Edwards and Kerry] have got a very limited view about how to use U.S. military forces to defend America. It's a consistent pattern over time of always being on the wrong side of defense issues.

And, finally, to Halliburton.

EDWARDS: We also thought it was wrong to have a $20 billion fund out of which $7.5 billion was going to go to a no-bid contract for Halliburton, the vice president's former company. It was wrong then. It's wrong now.

Edwards intentionally brought up Halliburton very early in the debate, "because I thought it undermined the vice president's credibility," he said later. "You know he was continuing to try and claim that he was concerned about ordinary people, concerned about the war, and I just thought that the whole issue of Halliburton and his history with Halliburton undermined his credibility."

Cheney deflected the Halliburton issue by charging that Edwards was only trying to obscure his and John Kerry's record. What riled him the most, however, was Edwards's mention of his daughter.

That came after Ifill asked Cheney about current administration policy on same-sex marriage in light of what he had said four years before: "Freedom means freedom for everybody."

CHENEY: Gwen, you're right, four years ago in this debate, the subject came up. And I said then and I believe today that freedom does mean freedom for everybody. People ought to be free to choose any arrangement they want. It's really no one else's business. That's a separate question from the issue of whether or not government should sanction or approve or give some sort of authorization, if you will, to these relationships.

Traditionally, that's been an issue for the states. States have regulated marriage, if you will. That would be my preference. . . .

EDWARDS: . . . Let me say first that I think the vice president and his wife love their daughter. I think they love her very much. And you can't have anything but respect for the fact that they're willing to talk about the fact that they have a gay daughter, the fact that they embrace her. It's a wonderful thing.

About that exchange, Cheney said later, "It was the way it came up, related to a family member, to talk about one of my children, that was the wrinkle that I thought was not in the best taste, if I can put it in those terms. I thought it was a bit of a cheap shot."

How did he handle his anger?

"Controlled it."

Edwards didn't see it as a cheap shot.

"I think he is just dead wrong. I honestly thought this was something to be admired. I thought the American people would respond really positively to what the vice president had done. I thought it was an example of a difference between the vice president and the president. That was the point I was making, because I agreed with what he had been doing within his family, and I didn't agree with what President Bush was doing."

Cheney believes that when Kerry brought up his daughter's sexual orientation in the second presidential debate it ultimately hurt the Kerry-Edwards cause.

From the moderator's perspective, Gwen Ifill told me that the anticipation of fireworks between Cheney and Edwards was difficult to deal with—at first.

"I was a near basket case myself going in because of the pressure I felt from moderating such a high-stakes event as that for the first time," she said. "But the candidates and their staffs were so much more tense and nervous than I was. . . . I felt better, I relaxed and I was fine."

She said she had absolutely no second thoughts about raising the same-sex marriage issue to Cheney in light of his "freedom means freedom for everybody" line four years before in the Lieberman debate.

As with Lieberman, there has been a major moving-on PS to John Edwards's candidacy for vice president—a heartbeat away from the most powerful job in the world. Edwards became a disgraced star of the tabloids after admitting in 2010 that he had a child out of wedlock with a campaign aide while his wife, Elizabeth, was being treated for breast cancer. The Edwardses divorced before Elizabeth died in December 2010.

Meanwhile, Dick Cheney became a hit of anti-Obama outspokenness on the Sunday-morning talk shows after leaving office in 2009 with the lowest poll approval ratings in history.

THE BUSH-KERRY debate in Miami spawned two unusual entertainment creations.

In 2005, I received a phone call from Lawrence O'Donnell, Jr., then one of the executive producers and writers for the NBC drama series *The West Wing*. He was—is—a man of many careers, having worked as an actor, a Senate staffer, and a political analyst on MSNBC.

His pitch to me was straightforward. He wanted me to moderate a live debate on *The West Wing* between their two fictional candidates for president—Arnold Vinick, the Republican nominee played by Alan Alda, and Matt Santos, the Democrat portrayed by Jimmy Smits.

My first reaction was pleasant, appreciative—and negative. It might be fun, sure, but there was no way I could do that. I am a journalist, not an actor. Besides, we have rules at *The NewsHour* against journalists doing such things—rules that I helped write.

O'Donnell said it would be done on a set that would be a virtual re-creation of the two-podium arrangement that marked the real event in Florida. Every detail would be replicated. It would not be completely scripted. I would have full editorial control of what questions I asked.

I was a longtime viewer and fan of *The West Wing*. I thought it was the first believable take on what went on in real Washington and the West Wing, the White House, and the U.S. Capitol. The characters and dialogue rang true.

O'Donnell asked if I had been following the current story line—the race to succeed the retiring president played by Martin

Sheen. Yes, pretty much so, I said. O'Donnell said he would overnight several DVDs of the most recent episodes, including one that had yet to air.

I heard myself telling him how much I admired the acting of the entire cast of *The West Wing*. I praised Smits, mentioning his performance on *NYPD Blue* as detective Bobby Simone. And Alan Alda, well, he was one of the great actors of our time.

We want the real thing, O'Donnell said. We want it to be a real debate. There would be few rules. The story line already called for the candidates to dramatically scrap them as the debate opened. The candidates could question and talk to each other directly. Would I at least consider doing it?

Okay, okay. Give me a day or two.

I ran it by Kate and the family, *NewsHour* leaders Les Crystal and Linda Winslow, and Robert MacNeil, my friend and retired partner. All of them pretty much reacted the same way. After a brief pause, each asked if I really wanted to. *That* question again. I gave some kind of answer that said yes, I guess I do. It could be terrific fun. MacNeil said I had earned the right to interpret our own rules however I wanted to. It could be justified on the grounds that it would be good publicity for *The NewsHour*.

I got only one strong are-you-nuts? reaction from a personal friend with both political and movie connections. The rest were more or less positive.

The next day I was ready to call O'Donnell with my happy acceptance. Then I came to my senses. I managed to grab my ego by my professional whatevers and told O'Donnell how much I appreciated being asked, but I could not do it. Nothing had changed. Journalists should not play themselves in movies or on TV dramas.

So on the night of November 6, 2005, Vinick/Alda debated Santos/Smits without me. Forrest Sawyer, a former network correspondent, was the moderator. All three did their respective jobs well. The subjects were real—Head Start, jobs, gun control, alternative energy sources, and leadership, among others. The exchanges and the debate itself did have a sound and feel of reality to them. O'Donnell and company, I thought, did an excellent job.

The format was wide-open after the candidates/actors agreed, right at the beginning, to drop all rules—just like Peter Jennings had suggested back in 1988.

Then came a ninety-minute one-act play called *The Strangerer* by Mickle Maher that premiered in 2007 at the Chopin Theater in Chicago and made an Off-Broadway run at the Barrow Street Theatre in New York the next year.

It had only three characters—George W. Bush, John Kerry, and me.

The set was a replica of the Miami debate stage. The actor playing me takes the moderator chair and then, on cue to an imaginary television camera, says exactly what I said in opening the real debate:

"Good evening from the University of Miami Convocation Center in Coral Gables, Florida—"

Following those and the rest of my real opening words, the actor playing Kerry gives the senator's real answer about how he believes he can make America safer than President Bush can. Then the stage directions take the drama in a surprising course:

[BUSH *takes out a knife and approaches* LEHRER'S *desk. He stabs* LEHRER *in the back.* LEHRER *collapses.* BUSH *steps back. Lights fade slowly to black, as a softly dramatic, melancholic theme plays over the sound of a rising wind. After a brief blackout: Lights up.* LEHRER *is back at his table, the candidates at their lecterns.*]

The Lehrer character says good evening again, welcomes everyone to the debate again, and explains that the knife used to stab "me" was not an actual knife. It was a prop.

Then Kerry is asked the "America safer" question again. As Kerry repeats his answer, there is a second stage direction.

[BUSH *pulls out a handgun, strides over to* LEHRER, *takes aim, and fires, once.* LEHRER *clutches his chest, gasps, falls on the floor.* BUSH *then fires four shots into his prostrate body.*]

So it goes.

The next time Bush comes up to me with a pillow.

[BUSH *has the pillow over* LEHRER'S *face. Pushes him down on the desk.* LEHRER *struggles, gets hold of the pillow, pulls away. There is a tug-of-war with pillow. Music continues, lights dimming still.*]

And so the play continues with dialogue based on the real debate itself interspersed with exchanges about various subjects such as beer, peanuts, *Who's Afraid of Virginia Woolf?,* and an evil witch named Rangda.

Later, "I" am served a glass of bourbon spiked with cyanide and then covered with gasoline to be burned to death. Kerry joins in the desire to kill the moderator before it's over.

But there was a bright side—a happy ending of sorts. According to the stage directions, when the lights dim for the last time at the curtain, "I" am still alive.

There seemed to be little agreement among reviewers—or even two members of my own family who saw it—about the play's merits or what exactly the play was about.

A New York reviewer said it was a play in the tradition of Edward Albee and Samuel Beckett. Another said it was inspired by the Albert Camus novel *The Stranger.*

The most memorable review line was: "It's the longest 90-minute play I've ever attended."

CHAPTER 7

Number Eleven

There is a theory that John McCain lost the 2008 election to Barack Obama at their first presidential debate on Friday, September 26, at the University of Mississippi, Oxford.

As with Richard Nixon in 1960 and Al Gore in 2000, that conclusion was not based on what McCain said.

McCain seemed nervous, fidgety, and on edge—at times, like George W. Bush in 2004, he came across as annoyed or semi-angry. He mostly refused even to look at Obama, despite the several invitations from the moderator—me—to do so. Obama, in contrast, came over as cool, relaxed, at ease. And he was more than willing to exchange words as well as looks with McCain.

The debate took place in an atmosphere that lived up to George H. W. Bush's "tension city" description. There was not even a possibility of gliding into the personal comfort zone that, after having moderated ten of these debates, I had come to relish—and depend on.

With two days to go, I was already in Oxford putting the

final touches to my questions—and thoughts—about the debate's agreed-to subject, foreign policy and national security, when the full wind from the financial crisis really hit.

Treasury Secretary Henry Paulson and Federal Reserve Chairman Ben Bernanke had proposed to Congress a $700 billion recovery plan a few days earlier. That followed the bankruptcy filing by Lehman Brothers, a leading investment bank. Bear Stearns had already been taken over by J. P. Morgan. Other major institutions—housing giants Fannie Mae and Freddie Mac, insurer AIG—were faltering. Credit was freezing, panic was spreading throughout the markets and the land.

McCain put his campaign on hold to return to Washington to deal with the situation—and the Paulson-Bernanke rescue proposal. He asked that the Oxford debate with Obama be delayed.

Obama said he was going to Oxford no matter what.

It was an easy call for me to quickly conclude that the scary economic developments had to be front and center on the debate, whenever it occurred. Never mind "foreign policy and national security." But I was no expert on financial matters, so I went on a crash course aimed at becoming comfortable asking such questions of the next president of the United States.

Another difficult mission was to consider how to deal with the possibility of a McCain no-show.

Through intermediaries, I was politely reminded that officials at the University of Mississippi and the citizens of Oxford had collected—and spent—several million dollars to prepare the town and the campus for a major national event. Also, several hundred people, including many students, were anticipating the "experience of a lifetime" of being in the live audience for a presidential debate.

I had been most impressed with how important this debate was to the people of the university and Oxford. The whole community—businesses and faces—were decorated and lit up by what was about to happen. Everyone in Oxford seemed part of the debate preparations and logistics. Kate and I had been provided a spacious apartment in a condominium. We rented a large private residence nearby for the rest of our family.

There finally came a semi-official plea. In order to save the situation a bit, would I be willing to moderate an Obama-only event of some kind, possibly in a town hall format with questions from students?

I began a round of consultations by phone with Janet Brown of the debate commission and, in person, with *NewsHour* executive producer Linda Winslow, who had come to Oxford as my professional "keeper/handler." Winslow, his longtime deputy, had replaced Les Crystal in both jobs.

I also spoke repeatedly and compulsively with Kate and our three daughters.

The principal issue for me was the old-fashioned one of not doing anything that had a whiff of favoring one side over another.

I wanted to know what the possible fallback positions were if the debate was rescheduled for another day in another city or town? There was also the question of whether the television networks, as well as PBS and the cable channels, would likely carry a solo Obama event. And, if not, what difference would it—should it—make?

And as I finally drifted off to sleep that night I began to consider how I would handle an Obama-only event. How should the questions from the students be handled? Stand up and ask them with no pre-screening? Write them down beforehand and then I select and read them out loud to Obama? How would that be decided—and by whom?

My wide-eyed wake-up question that next morning—debate day—was: Is McCain coming or not?

There was still no word when the family gathered for a walk to and around the town square, four blocks away.

We went into a men's clothing store. Whatever kind of event there was to be tonight, I had to carry out the debate necktie ritual. We were admiring the stock of blue-and-reds, in honor of the Ole Miss colors, when somebody in the store yelled out: "He's coming! I just heard it on the radio! McCain is coming!"

There will be a debate tonight! Hear ye! Hear ye! Hear ye!

I probably imagined it, but I swear I could pick up such cheers throughout the land of Oxford and greater Mississippi.

The only problem for me was that now I had to do it.

Just before 9 p.m. eastern time I sat at the ready.

As always, the copy was on a TelePrompTer mounted on a camera that was pointed directly toward me through a slot in the background set of the stage. Black fabric covered the camera to hide my big, bold white-on-black words from the TV or hall audience during the opening shots, particularly when the candidates came in, shook hands, and moved to their positions at the podiums.

The drill, which we had rehearsed more than once, was that

the black cloth would be removed during the countdown just before I was cued to begin.

In my earpiece, I heard the soft count from executive producer Marty Slutsky: "Ten, nine, eight, seven, six, five, four, three, two . . . go."

The background slit remained black—and blank. Somebody had forgotten to remove the cloth!

So, in a spurt of heroic, emergency ad-libbing, I said to Americans everywhere:

"Good evening from the Ford Center for the Performing Arts at the University of Mississippi in Oxford. I'm Jim Lehrer of *The NewsHour* on PBS, and I welcome you to the first of the 2008 . . ."

I reached for the paper script that was on the desk right in front of me, getting ready to read on. . . .

And then the black disappeared. Somebody had finally remembered to remove the cloth. The words came up and I read the rest of the opening on the prompter, thus ending the possibility of another personal crisis in presidential debate history.

I named the candidates and the commission as sponsors of this and the other debates to come, and said:

"Tonight's will primarily be about foreign policy and national security, which, by definition, includes the global financial crisis. It will be divided roughly into nine-minute segments. Direct exchanges between the candidates and moderator follow-ups are permitted after each candidate has two minutes to answer the lead question in an order determined by a coin toss. The specific subjects and questions were chosen by me. They have not been shared or cleared with anyone."

I moved on to the opening question but I did so poorly.

"Let me begin with something General Eisenhower said in his 1952 presidential campaign. Quote, 'We must achieve both security and solvency. In fact, the foundation of military strength is economic strength,' end quote."

It was a dumb and unnecessary justification for asking about the financial crisis. I also violated my own rules about getting right to the point. The words were barely out of my mouth when I thought about all the times I had shouted through a television screen to a moderator/interviewer, "Just ask the question!"

Finally, I did so.

"With that in mind, the first lead question:

"Gentlemen, at this very moment tonight, where do you stand on the financial recovery plan? First response to you, Senator Obama. You have two minutes."

OBAMA: Well, thank you very much, Jim, and thanks to the commission and the University of Mississippi, Ole Miss, for hosting us tonight. I can't think of a more important time for us to talk about the future of the country.

You know, we are at a defining moment in our history. Our nation is involved in two wars, and we are going through the worst financial crisis since the Great Depression.

And although we've heard a lot about Wall Street, those of you on Main Street I think have been struggling for a while, and you recognize that this could have an impact on all sectors of the economy. And you're wondering, how's it going to affect me? How's it going to affect my job? How's it going to affect my house? How's it going to affect my retirement savings or my ability to send my children to college?

So we have to move swiftly, and we have to move wisely. And I've put forward a series of proposals that make sure that we protect taxpayers as we engage in this important rescue effort. . . .

After a while, it was his opponent's turn.

LEHRER: Senator McCain, two minutes.

MCCAIN: Well, thank you, Jim. And thanks to everybody. And I do have a sad note tonight. Senator Kennedy is in the hospital. He's a dear and beloved friend to all of us. Our thoughts and prayers go out to the lion of the Senate. I also want to thank the University of Mississippi for hosting us tonight.

And, Jim, I—I've been not feeling too great about a lot of things lately. So have a lot of Americans who are facing challenges. But I'm feeling a little better tonight, and I'll tell you why. Because as we're here tonight in this debate, we are seeing, for the first time in a long time, Republicans and Democrats together, sitting down, trying to work out a solution to this fiscal crisis that we're in.

And have no doubt about the magnitude of this crisis. And we're not talking about failure of institutions on Wall Street. We're talking about failures on Main Street, and people who will lose their jobs, and their credits, and their homes, if we don't fix the greatest fiscal crisis, probably in—certainly in our time, and I've been around a little while.

But the point is—the point is, we have finally seen Republicans and Democrats sitting down and negotiating together and coming up with a package. This package has transparency in it. It has to have accountability and oversight. . . .

When both had finished their two minutes, I spoke again.

LEHRER: All right, let's go back to my question. How do you all stand on the recovery plan? And talk to each other about it. We've got five minutes. We can negotiate a deal right here. . . . Do you favor this plan, Senator Obama, and you, Senator McCain? Do you—are you in favor of this plan?

OBAMA: [*speaking directly to me*] We haven't seen the language yet. . . .

And he went on to attack the Bush administration's policies and corporate greed that led to the financial crisis and the failures of Fannie Mae and Freddie Mac, among other things.

LEHRER: [*to McCain*] . . . you're going to vote for the plan?

MCCAIN: [*speaking directly to me*] Sure. But—but let

me—let me point out, I also warned about Fannie Mae and Freddie Mac and warned about corporate greed and excess, and CEO pay. . . .

LEHRER: Do you have something directly to say, Senator Obama, to Senator McCain about what he just said?

OBAMA: [*looking back and forth between McCain and me*] Well, I think Senator McCain's absolutely right that we need more responsibility, but we need it not just when there's a crisis. I mean, we've had years in which the reigning economic ideology has been what's good for Wall Street, but not what's good for Main Street.

And there are folks out there who've been struggling before this crisis took place. And that's why it's so important, as we solve this short-term problem, that we look at some of the underlying issues. . . .

Obama was glancing at McCain, but his answer referred to McCain in the third person.

"Say it directly to him," I commanded.

Still not looking at McCain, Obama said, "I do not think that they [the economic fundamentals] are . . ."

"Say it directly to him," I urged again.

The formal, written rules for the debate, as negotiated and agreed to by the debate commission and the candidates, included a tricky wrinkle. For the first time in several election seasons candidates would be permitted to address and question each other directly.

I had assured commission officials that I would make a strong effort to facilitate that interaction, discouraging the then-prevailing practice of candidates mostly speaking only to the television camera or the moderator. I was keeping my promise.

Talking toward McCain, the next president of the United States did what he was told.

"Well, the—John, ten days ago you said that the fundamentals of the economy are sound. And—"

"Are you afraid I couldn't hear him?" McCain asked, looking right at me.

The audience laughed—and laughed.

I was sure the laughs were all directed at me.

"I'm just determined to get you all to talk to each other. I'm going to try."

Rightly or wrongly, I hung in there. A moment later, I asked McCain if he agreed with Obama about something.

"And if you don't, tell him what you disagree with."

McCain answered, but again he spoke and looked directly back at me—and the camera.

The pattern held for the remainder of the ninety minutes. While Obama often addressed McCain directly, referring to him as "John," McCain always looked either at the audience, the camera, or me.

The word "Barack" never passed his lips.

I had a feeling sitting there that night that McCain's refusal to address Obama directly, as well as McCain's tense body language, would affect the final outcome of the election.

Two of America's top political journalists, Dan Balz and

Haynes Johnson, came to a similar conclusion. In their 2009 book, *The Battle for America, 2008,* they called the Oxford debate the campaign's "turning point." The contrast between "a cool, composed" Obama and McCain, who "continually dismissed his opponent" and wouldn't even look at him, made the difference:

"It wasn't a knockout, but it seemed to signal the moment when Obama crossed the threshold to answer the 'is he ready' question."

Is he ready? That, I believe, is the question that underlies most moments of most presidential debates. At Oxford, Obama's and McCain's differences on the financial crisis, Iraq, terrorism, et al. were props for the main event—Cool versus Edge. For Kennedy-Nixon and Mondale-Reagan the comparative issue was charm, while human emotions were central to Dukakis-Bush I as was general likability to other encounters, most specifically Bush II against both Gore and Kerry.

There is a natural follow-up to the "ready" question, of course. How will he/she deal with the unexpected?

The Soviet Union sends missiles to Cuba. The Vietnam War escalates. Watergate gets covered up. Hostages are taken at the U.S. embassy in Tehran. Iraq invades Kuwait. Impeachment charges are filed. Terrorists fly airliners into U.S. buildings. Hurricane Katrina hits the Gulf. A deep-water oil rig explodes. . . .

Voters watch debates for candidates' body language and temperament—indications of how candidates might react under pressure, under severe testing. Some answers do come from direct statements about policy. But there were no debate questions in 1960 about Fidel Castro, for instance. And there were none in 2008 about possible threats from gigantic oil spills.

A speculative thought: Might Bill Clinton have been more careful in his personal life afterward if the women/character issue had been raised with more public force in the 1996 debates?

THERE HAVE YET to be any purposeful postmortem reflections about the 2008 debates from President Obama or Senator McCain, Vice President Joe Biden or Sarah Palin, the Republican vice presidential nominee.

Most of what either Obama or McCain has had to say was to reporters or in television appearances right afterward.

George Stephanopoulos on ABC's *This Week* noted to McCain that it seemed as if he was reluctant even to look at Obama during the Oxford debate.

"I wasn't," McCain said. "Of course not."

Stephanopoulos asked about commentators who suggested that he was showing disdain for Obama.

"I was looking at the moderator a great deal of the time. I was writing a lot of the time. I in no way know how that in any way would be disdainful. . . . I've been in many, many debates, and a lot of times I don't look at my opponents because I'm focusing on the people and the American people that I'm talking to. That's what a debate is all about."

Obama was interviewed by Bob Schieffer on CBS's *Face the*

Nation. Schieffer said Democrats had suggested McCain was being condescending to him.

Schieffer asked Obama if he believed that.

"Well, I think it was a debating trick, which is to essentially keep on asserting that because of my vast years in Washington somehow I'm better qualified to be president. And one of the points that I've made consistently in this campaign is that if the length of tenure in Washington is a measure of your wisdom, then people should vote for somebody else. But I think the American people understand that the conventional wisdom in Washington, which John McCain has followed for the last eight years, is exactly what needs to be changed."

More is bound to come out someday from the participants—in various memoirs, if not before.

There is also sure to be punditry galore forever about the Cool versus Edge choice of 2008. Less than two years into the Obama presidency there was already much talk about whether Obama had turned out to be *too* cool. Some of his political friends were even advising him openly to show more edge.

The Commission on Presidential Debates took another major step toward full autonomy in 2008—at least, as it involves the selection of moderators. The three besides me were Schieffer of CBS, Tom Brokaw of NBC, and Gwen Ifill of PBS.

The McCain and Obama campaigns were not told the four names until shortly before they were announced to the press by Janet Brown and the commission cochairs, Paul Kirk and Frank Fahrenkopf.

It had been twenty-four years since the opening of the first

1984 Reagan-Mondale debate at Louisville, Kentucky, when Barbara Walters lodged her very public complaint about the campaigns' power to veto moderators and panelists.

Kirk and Fahrenkopf, along with Janet Brown, are given much credit for the slow but sure move toward building the commission's independence. As former national party chairmen— Kirk, the Democrat, and Fahrenkopf, the Republican—they established a thin but firm line between representing the competing interests of their own parties' campaigns and of the commission. As politicians, they also knew about compromise.

All four 2008 moderators drew criticism for our respective labors. Whatever their merits, the accessibility of email and other rapid response electronics made critiques more plentiful than ever.

Most of mine were about the "stupid," "obsessive," or "school principal" manner in which I tried to get Obama and McCain to interact.

Guilty as charged.

Tom Brokaw moderated the McCain-Obama town hall debate on October 7, 2008, at Belmont University in Nashville, Tennessee. The critics accused him of bringing an anchorman's all-about-me approach to the debate, worrying more about asking his own questions than facilitating those of the ordinary citizens in the hall.

I had warned Brokaw that heat was coming no matter what. He talked afterward about that in an interview with my PBS colleague Tavis Smiley:

"Lehrer said, 'Fair warning. No one will be happy when it's over.' And I called him today and said, 'You could not have

warned me enough, it turns out.' But those are the consequences. I think the country is better off for it."

Bob Schieffer was the moderator of the third debate—a sit-
down event at Hofstra University in Hempstead, New York.
Most of the criticism of his work came from the predictable political opinion bloggers. Liberals/Democrats and conserva-
tives/Republicans, each in their own way, accused Schieffer of
favoring the other side.

Schieffer had confessed something to me after his maiden
debate, the 2004 Bush-Kerry event in Tempe, Arizona.

"I have been on television so often for so long I thought
there was no way in the world I would be nervous doing that
kind of thing. Oh, how wrong I was. I was shaking like a leaf as
I waited offstage for that to start."

I had those same kinds of experiences, although my
metaphors ran more along the lines of knife blades than leaves.

Gwen Ifill made some moderator history in the Palin-Biden
event at Washington University in St. Louis. In the language of
sports, she played hurt.

Three days before flying to St. Louis for the debate, she
tripped over some of her research material at her Washington,
D.C., home and broke her right ankle.

Were you in pain during the debate? I asked.

"Not a bit. The adrenaline was running. I didn't feel a
thing—until it was over."

Ifill had another pain to survive as well. A few days before
the debate, there was an announcement of a new book she was
writing titled *The Breakthrough: Politics and Race in the Age
of Obama*. Some bloggers and others suggested that the book

tainted her as a neutral moderator even though, as she said immediately, the book was not finished, particularly the ending that would deal with Obama specifically. It was just the title that upset some in the political world.

"The broken ankle, strange as it may seem, actually helped me get through that book storm," Ifill said. "Between dealing with that and preparing for the debate itself I had no time or energy to deal with what I considered to be an unfair attack on my integrity.

"Besides, I knew that whatever, it would all come out in the end with how I handled the debate itself and what was written in my book."

And that, of course, is exactly what happened. The critics went silent after both events and have remained so.

THERE IS AN intensely personal backstory about how I came to moderate one of the 2008 presidential debates—my eleventh.

A routine physical examination in April of that year turned up the fact that my aortic valve was deteriorating. It was serious enough to threaten congestive heart failure. My doctor Ramin Oskoui urged me to act quickly—to have open-heart surgery and replace the valve.

Kate and I, accompanied as always at key times by our daughters, went off to Massachusetts General Hospital in Boston to get the job done. There was some heightened risk because I had had an open-heart bypass operation in 1984 following a heart attack.

I was blessed by having two superb doctors on my case—

cardiologist Roman DeSanctis and heart surgeon Cary Akins. They went about the business of replacing my aortic valve with that of a pig. Both doctors assured me that "if all goes as expected" I would not only be all right, I would come out feeling and acting ten years younger.

I didn't believe a word of it, to tell the truth.

But, as it turned out, they were right. After a recovery period at home in Washington of just over two months, I was back to work on *The NewsHour* part-time and at the word processor writing my novels. It wasn't long afterward that I felt fully recovered—and then some.

And then came the call from Janet Brown of the debate commission. It was early—weeks before anything had been said publicly about the coming debates between McCain and Obama, beyond when and where they would be.

Brown, now a good friend, laid it out straight: "If asked by the commission to moderate one of the 2008 debates, would you do it?" (At *The NewsHour,* we call that a "seventh-grade prom question." "If I asked you to go to the prom with me, Natasha, would you go?")

I was not expecting the invitation. I had already concluded after 2004, separate from my life with the valve and the pig, that I had done my last debate.

But in spite of that, I did talk again to the family—and a few friends.

As before, the discussion was mostly about whether I really *wanted* to do it.

I ended up saying yes to Janet Brown—one more time. In doing so, I came up with several reasons, including the fact that it would demonstrate convincingly that I really had recovered from my heart operation.

I was no invalid, by God! I had already anchored our *NewsHour* coverage of the two national party conventions in August, in fact. . . .

Ego impulses aside, the real reason was that I wanted to do it. This was what I did. I was a moderator.

★

CHAPTER 8

Mr. Jefferson, Among Others

Moderators are not just for and about presidential debates, obviously.

"Good morning from Austin, Texas . . . and welcome to the National Issues Convention . . . an experiment in democracy based on the premise that information and dialogue on issues leads to deliberation, to informed opinions, and thus to informed voters."

Those were some of my opening words for one of the many other experiences that have yielded moderating rewards and strains.

The events have ranged from formal confrontations among the four leaders of the U.S. Congress and discussions of presidential character to the real beliefs of the founding fathers and an unprecedented public forum in Kansas City, Missouri, with the chairman of the Federal Reserve, Ben Bernanke. Some have been nationally televised; others have taken place before audiences in a variety of smaller venues.

Each, in its own way, has contributed to the learning and

other curves that never end for those who regularly moderate public exchanges of any kind or size.

My favorites include a discussion involving Thomas Jefferson and his manservant, and an extraordinary Cold War retrospective by François Mitterrand, Margaret Thatcher, Mikhail Gorbachev, Brian Mulroney, and George H. W. Bush.

That National Issues Convention in Austin was one of the hardest moderating jobs I have had. More than 400 citizens—466, to be exact—came together from all lifestyles, beliefs, and parts of the country for four days of talking and listening about what the 1996 presidential election should really be about. They were rich and poor, young and old, PhD's and dropouts, informed and isolated, happy and angry, advocates and listeners.

Their discussions began among themselves and moved on to include issue experts and, finally, leading political figures in the 1996 presidential race. More than nine hours of the convention's varied exchanges were broadcast live or on tape nationwide on PBS.

In an interesting precursory coincidence, the governor of Texas gave the welcoming remarks on Thursday night, and the vice president of the United States was the guest on that final "good morning" Sunday session.

They were, respectively, George W. Bush and Al Gore.

The heavy-duty centerpiece for the convention was a deliberative poll, called "the poll with a human face." The purpose was to discover if and how solid information, civil discussion, and serious deliberation can cause voters to alter their opinions.

Senator Richard Lugar was there in person, while other contestants for the Republican presidential nomination—Phil Gramm, Steve Forbes, and Lamar Alexander—joined by satellite on huge television monitors. Bob Dole, the early front-runner, hadn't even bothered to do that. Instead, he attended a campaign event at a Dartmouth College frat house in New Hampshire. (Seriously!)

While not part of any polling, deliberative or otherwise, the clear "winners" of the convention were Gore and Lugar, partly because they had actually shown up.

The Republican evening was three hours of moderator hell. Trying to facilitate coherent dialogue between delegates in the hall and the three airtime-hungry candidates via unstable satellite feeds, plus one who was physically present, was nightmarish. We repeatedly lost picture and, more important, the audio often cut in and out. That often forced me to repeat either a question or an answer—sometimes both—in order to keep the conversation going.

The faces of the three on giant screens often had a creepy Big Brother movie effect, particularly when the images flashed in and out of focus—or sight.

Lugar scored the highest, not simply because he was there but because he came across as a man of quiet intelligence and grace.

Gore's one-hour Sunday morning session was a clear win for him. Knowing that the Clinton-Gore ticket was already way ahead in the polls against any potential Republican slate no doubt contributed to his relaxed and confident demeanor. He drew the delegates into easy back-and-forths.

There was an overwhelming consensus among the 466

people afterward that the simple exercise of being in the same room in listening mode with such a diverse group was exhilarating—in some cases, life changing.

My own favorite episodes involved a young black mother on welfare—a Democrat—and a middle-aged white businessman—a Republican. Neither had ever been in the real company of the other before, much less had a conversation as they were forced to do in their small group. After some initial and quite natural reluctance to deal with each other, they started talking—and listening.

When it was over, the man spoke with me and others about how "welfare mothers" really cared more about their children than getting government handouts—something he hadn't really believed before. The woman mused about the man's point that the constitution ensures equal opportunity but not outcomes.

"That was the single best event of its kind I have ever been involved in," said Al Gore a week later at a small luncheon in the Old Executive Office Building next to the White House. The lunch was a traditional one on State of the Union day for television anchors who would be covering the speech that night. Gore's enthusiasm for what happened in Austin forced my friends Tom Brokaw, Dan Rather, and Peter Jennings to hear all about it. And I loved that.

I felt the same way Al Gore did about the event itself. I, too, had never seen anything quite like it. It was so unique because the debating followed a sharing about one another as well as the issues. The discourse was truly—and neutrally—informed.

STAGED UNDER THE auspices of Colonial Williamsburg, my event with Mr. Jefferson took place before five thousand people in August 2009 at the Chautauqua Institution, the famous summer performance and lecture center in western New York State. Jefferson, played by Colonial Williamsburg's regular actor Bill Barker, appeared with Jupiter, his servant slave, portrayed by Richard Josey.

I had not told Barker and Josey what I was going to ask them, except that it would be mostly about slavery and freedom. I was most impressed and fascinated with the realistic way these two men brought Jefferson and Jupiter so much to life and thought. They were in eighteenth-century dress sitting on a stage with me, like in any other two-guest discussion.

I asked Jupiter if he saw himself as a person or a slave.

"I see you as a man and I am the same," Jupiter responded, looking at me. "My status as Negro in these colonies by the law is to be a slave to others. That is the nature of things."

I asked Jefferson what it means to him to own a slave.

He said he seldom referred to them as slaves. "They are my people," adding that he personally believed slavery was disgraceful and that he had always been at work to abolish the slave trade.

Jefferson declined to confirm that he had fathered children with slaves.

Jupiter said, "There are no children on Monticello that are fathered by Mr. Jefferson. There is nothing more that I can give you today, sir, than I have given you, and that is the truth."

I'VE HAD A long relationship with Colonial Williamsburg that springs, among other delights, from my having served on its foundation board of trustees for many years.

It was in the restored House of Burgesses chamber there in 1996 that I moderated a special called *PBS Debate Night,* the first—and, as far as I know, only—public debate ever among the four top leaders of Congress.

Then Senate majority leader Trent Lott, Senate minority leader Tom Daschle, House Speaker Newt Gingrich, and House minority leader Richard Gephardt went at it for ninety minutes.

My favorite exchange came over who could best manage the work of the Congress—Democrats or Republicans? It culminated in Gingrich's boast that he had saved the taxpayers $500,000 a year by eliminating the fourteen full-time jobs of those who delivered buckets of ice to House members twice a day.

A much broader Williamsburg event in November 2007 was part of an ongoing PBS program/project called *By the People*. It brought a varied cast of fifty people from around the country to talk about the duties of citizenship in the twenty-first century.

The participants included craigslist founder Craig Newmark, Indianapolis 500 race car driver Janet Guthrie, saxophonist Branford Marsalis, Illinois attorney general Lisa Madigan, Episcopal bishop Nathan Baxter, National Rifle Association executive Millie Hallow, evangelical minister Joel Hunter, U.S. Army major Ray Kimball, playwright David Henry Hwang, Arizona rancher Bill McDonald, and the mayors of Youngstown, Ohio, and Nebraska City, Nebraska.

At a Williamsburg event for a PBS special called *Character*

Above All, nine historians, writers, and journalists sat around the House of Burgesses benches discussing presidential character. Each participant had general expertise or special knowledge of one or more modern-day presidents.

They were Stephen Ambrose, Michael Beschloss, Ben Bradlee, Robert Dallek, Hendrik Hertzberg, James Cannon, David McCullough, Peggy Noonan, and Tom Wicker. Seldom, if ever, has so much wisdom about the presidency been assembled under one roof.

One sampling from Dallek:

Washington and Jefferson and Lincoln and FDR and TR and Wilson, Kennedy, Truman. They were great characters. They were great personalities. They were all larger than life. They impress themselves on our historical memory, and maybe there's a mythological quality to each of them and maybe that is an essential requirement of it. But there is a special presidential quality to all of this and it has to do with vision and constancy and courage and also practical good sense, pragmatism. Every one of these great presidents was also a great pragmatist, I think.

I learned a special moderating lesson at a September 2007 forum at Colonial Williamsburg.

Three supreme Early American historians—Gordon Wood, Hunter Rawlings, and Joe Ellis—discussed what the founding fathers had in mind as an end product for their creation.

A combination of breaking news events and poor personal

scheduling had left me in a car on the way from Washington to Williamsburg that morning without a forum question in my head.

So I just scribbled a list of "things." Most were simple one- or two-word descriptions of issues the founders *might* have considered as they debated forming a new independent nation from thirteen breakaway British colonies.

I, of course, had no idea how Wood, Rawlings, and Ellis would respond. I had read a few of their books and I knew them personally, but that was as close as I was to the enterprise, which a prestigious crowd was expected to attend.

Within ten minutes of getting out of the car, I was on a stage in a large auditorium sorting out my thoughts about the upcoming discussion.

The first subject on my list was "strong central government." Did the founders have such a concept in mind?

Wood, Rawlings, and Ellis gave brilliant answers.

"Independent judiciary" was next. What was their thinking about that?

Thereafter I moved the three great men of history on through "role of the presidency," "type of economic system," "taxes," "standing army and navy," "individual rights," "slavery," "God," "free press," "health care," "education," and "foreign policy."

To my own pleasure and amazement, the give-and-take among my three panelists—geniuses, I now think of them forever—was extraordinary. Not knowing what each was going to say, I was as freshly informed as the audience as I listened to each piece of information and insight about the founders' intent.

The bottom line for me was that I had escaped embarrassment, despite having violated a critical rule of moderating: Do your homework.

I have not always been so fortunate.

ON APRIL 16, 2002, with the tragedies of 9/11 still fresh, there was a panel discussion in the Spring Luncheon series at the New York Public Library. A full house of some four hundred or so library supporters was present for the event sponsored by the library's active volunteers program.

The subject was "America: What's Next?" The participants were *Washington Post* foreign affairs columnist Jim Hoagland, presidential historian Michael Beschloss, *New Yorker* staff writer and author Nicholas Lemann, and novelist-poet Jamaica Kincaid.

I was the moderator.

I had done very little preparation, because I had spent hours covering stories and running discussions on *The NewsHour* about the various impacts 9/11 was having and would continue to have on all levels of American society. I assumed the library discussion would be mostly reactive and, in many ways, an expansion of the layers of shared sadness, grief, and fear we all had as Americans.

I did go over the biographies of the panelists—I was already familiar with Beschloss and Hoagland—but did no further research on specifically what any of the four was likely to say.

That was my first mistake.

My second was to make a decision for strictly politically

correct reasons. Here we had—counting me—four white males and one black female. So on that basis alone I began the questioning with Jamaica Kincaid.

I have been unable to locate a transcript or recording of the discussion, but my memory and those of others has me asking a simplistic general question about the meaning of 9/11.

Jamaica Kincaid's immediate answer went right to what she had come to say: The people of New York City, if not all of America, must realize they deserve some of the blame for the attacks. Our militaristic, discriminatory, bullying attitudes and holier-than-thou righteousness, among other things, had essentially brought it all on ourselves.

I could hear and feel a whoosh of collective gasps from the audience. Several people stood up and walked out.

Beschloss, sitting on my left, whispered to me that it didn't matter what any of us say for the rest of this panel "because the audience will remember this one thing from the event."

He was absolutely right.

And the whole thing was my fault. First, I should have done my homework enough to know what Kincaid had on her mind to say. Then, PC or not, I should have gotten the discussion started on a more general track before opening the bomb bay for Kincaid. Her point would have still been heard loudly and clearly but within a context.

Since I was not prepared for her strong statement, I sputtered and stammered to get other answers in response. Hoagland quickly disputed Kincaid's premise. Beschloss took a similar position. And Lemann, on his way to becoming the dean of the Columbia University Journalism School, made a strong personal statement about the emotional impact the 9/11 attacks had had on the people of New York. The audience applauded.

The event struggled on for sixty minutes or more, making it one of the longest hours ever for me as a moderator, with my face remaining the warmest it has ever been during such an event.

In the end, there was no serious exchange of ideas. Kincaid's opening blast had devastated the audience and set the tone for the discussion that followed. And I was unable, through questions or other means, to get beyond it.

The point of the story is simply that I failed as a moderator, primarily because I did not go into it prepared.

It definitely was not Jamaica Kincaid's fault. She had a perfect right to say anything she wished. The responsibility was mine to make it work.

My face reddens with the retelling even now.

BUT I RETAIN a different kind of glow from the October 9, 1995, discussion among François Mitterrand, Margaret Thatcher, Mikhail Gorbachev, Brian Mulroney, and George H. W. Bush at the Broadmoor Hotel in Colorado Springs, Colorado.

The occasion was a private summit called "A World Transformed: Our Reflections on Ending the Cold War." Former president George H. W. Bush was the host; the George Bush Presidential Library Foundation and the Forum for International Policy were the sponsors. The invited audience of more than one hundred was made up of Bush friends, former officials of his administration, and supporters of his library, which was then under construction at Texas A&M University in College Station.

For several hours, divided among sessions over two days, the former prime ministers of Great Britain and Canada and the former presidents of France, the Soviet Union, and the United States talked in detail about their involvement in events and decisions that began with perestroika and went through the various revolutions in Eastern Europe, ending with the fall of the Berlin Wall.

To say that I "moderated" their discussion is not a precisely accurate description. Most of my questions were along the lines of "Is that how *you* saw it?" and followed longish statements, particularly by Gorbachev and Thatcher.

But that was way, *way* beside the point.

The pleasure for Kate and me and for all others present was to hear such things as Gorbachev recalling the first perestroika talks between American and Soviet officials.

"I would not want to paint a perfect picture. We sometimes had quite heated arguments, and I was sometimes struck by the fact that our ideas were not properly appreciated among those in the United States, including among people close to the president," Gorbachev said, referring to then president Ronald Reagan. "Some of them were saying that it was another Communist trick."

Mitterrand said, "What brought everything down was East Germany. They could not control the fantastic migration outflow from East Germany into Hungary, Czechoslovakia, and West Germany."

The former French president had already been diagnosed with the cancer that would cause his death three months later. His skin was gray and his body was frail, but his mind was as sharp as ever.

Thatcher was her usual Thatcher.

"You could not say it [the end of the Cold War] was inevitable," she said, among other things, disagreeing with Mitterrand. "It wasn't. It was facilitated."

She expressed a particularly dim view of Germans and reunification:

"I, to this day, cannot understand why so many Germans, who are so highly intellectual, let Hitler do the things he did. . . .

"There is something in the character of the German people which led to things that should never have happened. Some people say, 'You have got to anchor Germany into Europe to stop this feature from ever coming out again.' You have anchored Europe to a new dominant large Germany. . . .

"In the end, my friends, it will not work."

Thatcher drew a sharp response from Gorbachev with her claim that the missile defense proposal by Reagan—the Strategic Defense Initiative, or SDI, as it was called—helped bring an end to the Cold War.

"We could find a response to SDI, as well," Gorbachev said. "So SDI was not decisive in our movement toward a new relationship."

One of the most memorable Thatcher moments for me came at a small cocktail party for the major players before a larger prelude dinner.

President Bush took me over to one side within minutes after it began. "Guess what," he said with a friendly laugh. "My friend Maggie's got some strong ideas about how this thing is supposed to go in the morning. I told her it was your show and she should talk to you about it. Good luck, Jim." And he slapped me on the back and walked away.

Before I could take a breath or a first sip of wine, there was the former prime minister of Britain right by me.

"Now, here's what we must do," she said, with no real preamble. I did not write down her instructions and I do not remember them precisely, but it was mostly a list of what she thought were the *real* causes of the end of the Cold War that *must* be discussed.

I mumbled some kind of response and she went away.

Afterward, President Bush, who only three years before had lost his 1992 reelection run to Bill Clinton, brought the summit to an emotional close. Tears filled his eyes as he thanked his four fellow conferees:

"I loved our discussion. I so much miss this kind of thing. . . ."

He could not finish the sentence.

CHAPTER 9

★

Good Nights

"Thank you and good night."

Those words, addressed to a TV camera or to a room full of people, are an "off" switch for me. Done! The knife-blade trip is over. Now I can breathe normally again.

And begin to cherish the good but—mostly—to lament the bad.

Much *un*happiness came after the New York Public Library discussion. I had done a lousy job and I knew it. I also felt down after the three Bush-Gore debates in 2000 because of the overall mix of things—and having been whacked in *The New York Times*.

But so it always goes.

Some moderating mishaps are truly unavoidable—and un-chargeable, so to speak, to the moderator: an audio line goes dead, a TelePrompTer stays dark, a Secret Service agent blocks the path to the debate stage.

The ones that hurt are those where bad judgment and/or poor preparation caused the calamity. Both played a part, for example, in the library fiasco. I look upon the good end result of the discussion with the Colonial Williamsburg historians as an undeserved miraculous escape.

Preparation normally works on several levels for a moderator. Hard editorial research—homework—is critical for forming questions, but there is more to it than that. Homework is also the route to confidence: to know that whatever happens, mechanically or intellectually, *I* can deal with this, whether a candidate violates the rules, a question bombs, or a sentence comes out incomprehensibly.

I have in my ancient journalist mind what I call "the click." It began for me nearly fifty years ago as a newspaper reporter in Texas, and I have carried it with me as the guiding force in my work in journalism ever since.

The click comes when I know I am ready. Sometimes it happens almost immediately after I conduct one or two interviews or gather a few pieces of information; sometimes it comes later. And sometimes the click never comes. The story is not ready and may never be.

Today, the click mostly signifies that I am in my zone ready to sit across from somebody or a group of somebodies and conduct a fair and fruitful exchange.

For a presidential or vice presidential debate, the search for the click is long and hard. It is the grail behind every moment I spend preparing for a debate. Until that click comes, I am not fit to live with and not easy on my colleagues, family—or myself.

A most critical aspect of the click has to do with listening to the answers. If my preparation is limited to only writing questions, there will be no click—no real one. Most anyone, even ten people off the street, as they say, can think up some form of question.

Not everyone can be relaxed or comfortable enough to seriously listen to the answers.

As I see it, the airwaves of America are chock-full of television and radio people who ask memorized precisely worded questions and then seemingly ignore the answers and move on to another prepared question.

From the click comes an attitude for listening that is not only sensitive to follow-up possibilities but also to engagement, which I believe is essential for any real public exchange to work.

The language between and among the parties should be that of the body as well as the mouth. Nods of agreement, head shakes of disagreement, frowns, and smiles are all part of such an effective exercise. There is nothing more disconcerting to a participant, for instance, than to answer a question while the interviewer is looking away or down at a paper for the next question.

That is one of the reasons that I always—always—do my best to keep my eyes—and mind—on the one talking. Yes, it did lead me to miss the Big Sigh news of the first Gore-Bush debate in Boston, but the trade-off was worth it.

There's a made-up example I often use in speeches to explain the hazards of not paying attention to what is being said:

Q: Senator, do you believe the U.S. should sell more grain to Cuba?

A: Yes, Jim, I do. But first we should bomb Havana.

Q: What kind of grain, Senator?

There was a very public real-world reminder of the listen/follow-up challenge in January 2010. Former New York City mayor Rudy Giuliani was talking on ABC's *Good Morning America* about the 2009 Christmas Day bombing attempt on an airliner bound for Detroit.

"We had no domestic attacks under Bush," said Giuliani, referring to former president George W. Bush. "We've had one under Obama."

The interviewer, George Stephanopoulos, moved on to another subject without first noting—for Giuliani and the audience—that Bush was president when the September 11, 2001, attacks occurred. There were other Bush-era terror incidents as well, including the shoe-bombing attempt on an airliner flying to the United States from London.

The New York Times, following the lead of several bloggers, jumped on the Stephanopoulos story. He answered on his own blog:

"All of you who have pointed out that I should have pressed him on that misstatement in the moment are right. My mistake, my responsibility."

MY MISTAKE, MY responsibility.

Honest, professional words that must be at the ready for all of us who interview and moderate.

I have a personal example that is much worse than George's.

It happened during my interview with then president Bill Clinton on January 21, 1998, that day in infamy when the Monica Lewinsky story broke.

I had a long-scheduled conversation with Clinton to preview his coming State of the Union address. The White House had agreed to at least thirty minutes, to be taped at 1 p.m. in the Roosevelt Room next to the Oval Office for broadcast that evening. It was a significant coup for me and *The NewsHour.*

With the help of *NewsHour* editorial and research staff, I had spent hours studying the ramifications of the pope's visit to Cuba, which had just begun, as well as cramming about Bosnia, the Middle East, the Asian financial crisis, racial tensions, and affirmative action. I went to bed that night feeling prepared. I had done my homework.

The click had come.

At dawn's early light, I went out to get the morning newspapers from our front steps.

Across the top of *The Washington Post* was the headline: CLINTON ACCUSED OF URGING AIDE TO LIE.

I reacted with a two-word shout, the first word being "holy."

I quickly read the lead paragraph:

"Independent counsel Kenneth W. Starr has expanded his investigation of President Clinton to examine whether Clinton and his close friend Vernon Jordan encouraged a 24-year-old former White House intern to lie to lawyers for Paula Jones about whether the intern had an affair with the president, sources close to the investigation said yesterday."

Paula Jones was a former Arkansas state employee who had sued Clinton in civil court for allegedly sexually harassing her when he was governor.

Now I uttered another two or three words, none of which is repeatable, in the early morning quiet.

And I knew I was about to have one of the most important interviews of my small career or, more likely, no interview at all.

There was, in fact, considerable uncertainty between the *NewsHour* and White House staffs for the next few hours before we were given a final go.

At the request of ABC News and then of the other networks, we even agreed to allow everyone in the broadcast world to take the interview live. Our commercial colleagues were amazed that we had not held on to it as an "exclusive," only to be aired by us at a time of our choosing. *NewsHour* executive producer Les Crystal and I made the decision on the grounds that we of public broadcasting had a special obligation to share. I remain most pleased—and, yes, even proud—of what we did.

At 3:20 p.m. the first major post-Lewinsky-news interview with President Clinton was under way. We of *The NewsHour* saw it as a kind of coup of coups.

LEHRER: Mr. President, welcome.

CLINTON: Thank you, Jim.

LEHRER: The news of this day is that Kenneth Starr, independent counsel, is investigating allegations that you suborned perjury by encouraging a twenty-four-year-old woman, a former White House intern, to lie under oath in a civil deposition about her having had an affair with you. Mr. President, is that true?

CLINTON: That is not true. That is not true. I did not ask anyone to tell anything other than the truth. There is no improper relationship and I intend to cooperate with this inquiry, but that is not true.

So far, so good. Or so I thought at that most hairy, scary moment.

LEHRER: No improper relationship, define what you mean by that.

CLINTON: Well, I think you know what it means. It means that there is not a sexual relationship, an improper sexual relationship or any other kind of improper relationship.

LEHRER: You had no sexual relationship with this young woman?

CLINTON: There is not a sexual relationship. That is accurate. We are doing our best to cooperate here, but we don't know much yet, and that's all I can say now. What I'm trying to do is to contain my natural impulses and get back to work. It's important that we cooperate. I will cooperate, but I want to focus on the work at hand.

LEHRER: Just for the record, make sure I understand what your answer means and there is no ambiguity about it—

CLINTON: There is no ambiguity.

There was then an exchange in which Clinton said again he had not urged Lewinsky or anyone else, including his friend Vernon Jordan, to say anything that was not true. He repeated the

"There is no improper relationship" line and said all he knew about what was going on was what he had read in the newspapers. He said he'd been up late that night before talking about the Middle East and there were many serious matters on his presidential plate at the moment.

I finally decided Clinton was not going to go any further on the Lewinsky matter, so I moved on to the fact that the pope, along with the three network television anchors, were in Cuba.

"Has the time come maybe for the United States to also bury some economic and political hatchets with Cuba?" I asked.

And I reluctantly left the subject of one of the biggest political stories of our time and moved on to Cuba and other foreign policy issues in the Middle East and Bosnia, and then on to domestic matters.

I did come back to the Lewinsky story at the very end.

LEHRER: We're sitting here in the Roosevelt Room in the White House. It's 4:15 eastern time. All of the cable news organizations have been full of this story all day. The newspapers are probably going to be full of it tomorrow. And the news may—this story—is going to be there and be there and be there. The Paula Jones trial coming up in May. And you're going to be—

CLINTON: I'm looking forward to that.

LEHRER: Why?

CLINTON: Because I believe that the evidence will show what I have been saying; that I did not do what I was accused of doing.

There was a final minute during which, personal allegations aside, Clinton said he believed the American people should keep in mind all that he had done as president in the best interests of the country.

Then came the it's-over! words:

LEHRER: Mr. President, thank you very much.
CLINTON: Thank *you*.

Back at my office twenty minutes later, I called my wife, Kate. She said good things about my interview and then, after a whisk of a pause, told me that Amanda, one of our three grown daughters, had called to say the same.

"But she also wanted you to know that Clinton was using the present tense through much of what he said to you. He said 'is' in answering your relationship questions."

I had never before felt such a sense of calamitous failure and embarrassment. As in the case of the fictional question about bombing Havana, I had missed *it*. Yes, I was under much pressure and I had a lot on my mind, but there was no excuse for not having heard the word "is" in Clinton's answers.

A simple "Why are you using the present tense, Mr. President?" would have been a terrific follow-up.

Clinton's famous "It all depends on what you mean by 'is' " line came out the next day, as well as later during his impeachment and an unsuccessful attempt to remove him from office.

My mistake, blessedly, escaped attention because it got lost in the enormousness of the story itself. That was also before there were things called blogs.

For most everyone, that January 1998 day was about

history. For me it was about not being relaxed and/or confident enough to listen.

THEN THERE ARE the questions themselves.

I believe there's only one principal guideline for anyone who asks questions in public: Keep it simple.

The best example is what CBS correspondent Roger Mudd asked Senator Edward Kennedy in a November 1979 documentary. Kennedy was preparing to oppose President Jimmy Carter for the 1980 Democratic nomination.

"Why do you want to be president?" Mudd asked Kennedy.

Kennedy's face first went blank, then he remained absolutely silent with a puzzled look for a count of one, two, three. Finally, he said:

> KENNEDY: Well, I'm—were I to make the announcement to run, the reasons that I would run is because I have a great belief in this country that it is—has more natural resources than any nation of the world, has the greatest educated population in the world, the greatest technology of any country in the world, the greatest capacity for innovation in the world and the great political system in the world. . . .
>
> We're facing complex issues and problems in this nation at this time, but we have faced similar challenges at other times, and the energies and the resourcefulness of this nation, I think, should be focused on these prob-

lems that we face, primarily the issues on the economy, the problems of inflations, and the problems of energy, and I would basically feel that it's imperative for this country either [to] move forward, but it can't stand still or otherwise it moves backward.

MUDD: What would you do different from Carter?

KENNEDY: Well, in which particular areas?

MUDD: Well, just take the question of leadership.

KENNEDY: Well, it's—on what—on, you know, you have to come to grips with the different issues that we're facing. I mean we can—we'd have to deal with each of the various questions that we're talking about, whether it's questions of the economy, whether it's in the areas of energy.

Kennedy's candidacy against Carter never quite recovered from that exchange with Mudd.

James Fallows, in a September 2008 piece for *The Atlantic,* critiqued the three months of presidential primary debates as a prelude to what might be coming in the general election that fall. There were twenty-six among the Democrats, twenty-one for the Republicans.

And there were forty different moderators.

Fallows offered a list of the "Five Questions That Should Never Be Asked" that included two that I would give a special underlining—gotcha and loaded hypothetical.

Forget gotcha altogether. They are mostly for kids and amateurs.

Hypothetical questions can trigger a revealing answer, but they are easy to dodge and often result in criticism of the questioner. Bernard Shaw's killer question to Michael Dukakis remains the cardinal example of it playing out both ways.

I have already highlighted my own apples/oranges issues and long preface problems.

Also, forget multiple-choice or multiple-subject questions and those that are designed to show off how smart you are.

More generally, I would advise interviewers/moderators to treat the questionee with the same courtesy and respect you would want if you were being questioned. I would tell anyone who wishes to prosecute people on television to stay out of journalism and away from moderator chairs/tables. Instead, go for a job as an assistant district attorney—in the real or fictional worlds.

And I would urge all to never forget that one listener's stupid question can be another's brilliant one. Unfair? Not to me. Too long? Not long enough. Too incendiary? Not hot enough. Too gotcha? Not gotcha enough . . .

One critic's "sherry hour" way of questioning people could be another's ideal.

Some of the worst of all public questioners are members of the U.S. Congress. In particular, senators at televised hearings are too often in a subprime class by themselves.

New York Times columnist Gail Collins wrote a satirical piece on the 2009 hearings for Associate Justice Sonia Sotomayor, then a federal appeals court judge. Collins went through the hearings day by day giving examples—only barely fictional—of what the senators said.

"Senator Arlen Specter: Before we get to my questions, I would like to tell you several anecdotes about my own interesting history. Did I mention that I used to be chairman of this committee?"

"Senator Sessions: Judge, to get back to that 'wise Latina' speech, I want to know if you think judges should allow their prejudices to impact decision making. For instance, if I were a plaintiff before your court, would you be less inclined to rule in my favor because my middle name is Beauregard?"

"Senator Graham: Judge, before I read a string of anonymous comments about your temperament problem, I'd like to make you repeat that wise Latina remark again just for the heck of it."

Generally, the Democrats on the committee asked only questions that were helpful to Sotomayor, the nominee of a Democratic president, while the Republicans stayed on critical themes. In the 2005 hearings for Republican president George W. Bush's high court nominees John Roberts and Samuel Alito, the reverse was true. Democrats asked the tough ones; Republicans tossed the lobs.

According to the *Los Angeles Times* and several blogs, a word count of the four days of Sotomayor hearings showed 66 percent of them—95,592, to be exact—were spoken by senators, 34 percent—49,176—by the nominee.

There was a post-Sotomayor cartoon by William Haefeli in the August 10, 2009, issue of *The New Yorker* that said it all. A congressional hearing witness says to a questioner:

"I'm happy to answer your question as soon as you stop asking it."

———

SEVERAL TECHNIQUES WERE tested during the many television debates among Democratic and Republican primary candidates, particularly in 2008. Most, but not all, were on cable television.

They ranged from variations of the open approach to the use of taped citizen questions from YouTube. They even encouraged competing screams from rally-like audiences and gave birth to a series of "Raise your hand" candidate questions by moderators. ("Raise your hand if you believe there is such a thing as a global war on terror.")

James Fallows, in his *Atlantic* critique, said the most amazing thing about the Raise-your-hand stunt questions was the sheer indignity of it for the candidates.

"While candidates are subjected to almost everything during a long primary season and are used to skepticism and outright hostility from the press," he wrote, "serving as game-show props represented something new."

Among the other inexcusable situations during those 2008 primary debates, to my moderator eyes and ears, were when the candidates were not treated the same. The big names got center position onstage and more airtime than the others. The basics about the viability of any given candidate should be resolved during the invitation phase, not onstage.

Any candidate who meets the test to be invited deserves to be treated as all others.

The best primary debate I ever witnessed was in 1992 among six candidates for the Democratic nomination—Paul Tsongas,

Bob Kerrey, Tom Harkin, Jerry Brown, Douglas Wilder, and Bill Clinton. Robert MacNeil and I sat around a large round table in our Washington television studio with the candidates in what was essentially an open discussion that was lively, fairly enforced, and naturally fascinating.

THE LONG-HELD dream of a moderator-less debate remains unfulfilled. Since even before Kennedy-Nixon, there were advocates of what some labeled the "pure" format for presidential candidates.

All would give some kind of opening statement and then go directly at each other with questions and responses for ninety minutes or so, with the expectation that the candidates would be civic-minded enough to keep the times and tones fair and civilized.

It hasn't happened yet except in some early primary debates. But don't hold your breath that it will happen at the general election level, although a tiny—minuscule, let's say—step toward that was proposed and approved for the first Obama-McCain debate in Oxford. Its unprecedented rules permitted the candidates to address and question each other.

As debate scholars have pointed out, the advocates of the so-called real debates usually cite the seven Lincoln-Douglas debates as the purist model. But myths have grown up about those seven encounters.

They were organized by two Chicago newspapermen—Joseph Medill and Charles Ray—who were open supporters of Lincoln. After each debate, Medill and Ray made sure the press coverage was full and favorable to Lincoln. In other words, it was a 2008-like media-run exercise, complete with post-debate spinning and pre-debate negotiations.

On format, Lincoln and Douglas each gave an opening statement of either an hour or an hour and a half and then asked each other very long questions that drew very long answers.

Whatever the mythmakers say about the Lincoln-Douglas debates, in today's world they would probably be called back-to-back speeches, not debates.

There was a brief sideshow among some in journalism a few years ago over whether the televised presidential debates should even be called debates. Dan Rather, when he was with CBS, made a public point of always calling them "joint appearances" on the grounds that they were not real debates.

Regardless of what the event is called, the format, or the rules, democracy is always served any time candidates for the presidency or vice presidency of the United States are on the same stage at the same time talking about things that matter.

I feel the same way about public debates and discussions of every kind and level.

My advice to all with the power to choose is to fit the format to the specific event and its purpose. Sitting at a round table may be the best way to go. Or do it at podiums. Or have several people ask questions. Or only one or two. Perhaps open it up to the audience. . . .

Such decisions really can make a difference on how effective the experience can be for the participants as well as the audience.

Debates, with a variety of formats, are now a fact of presidential politics. And that is a good thing, according to what most of the candidates said in our documentary interviews.

The big exception was George H. W. Bush, the man who called the debates "ugly."

I asked if he thought they should be a *required* part of the process.

"No, I think you ought to do what's best to get you elected. And if that's best that you have no debates, too bad for all you debate-lovers because I really think a candidate should be entitled to that."

A similar attitude dominated the politics of Britain, a country with a grand tradition of debates—from Parliament and college unions to street corners. Prime ministers repeatedly dismissed televised debate challenges from opposition party leaders on grounds that they were stunts from losers. Incumbents and winners had nothing to gain by such encounters.

Then came 2010. Prime Minister and Labour Party leader Gordon Brown, à la Gerald Ford against Jimmy Carter in 1976, was behind in the opinion polls. Brown agreed to three ninety-minute debates with Conservative leader David Cameron and Nick Clegg, the head of the Liberal Democrats. The rules of engagement, like the provocation, were based on the American model. The three moderators were television anchormen who did mostly traffic-cop duties. The questions were asked by carefully chosen audience members in a town hall atmosphere.

Brown ended up losing his Labour majority and resigning as prime minister. Would it have turned out differently if there had been no televised debates? *That* debate will likely continue until there is another national election debate challenge.

Some of the heavy British press buildup to the 2010 debates centered on the American experience. In the course of a few interviews, I was asked for advice I might have for the British participants.

For the moderators, I recommended that their success be judged by how invisible they were. For the candidates: Whatever you do, answer the question.

FINALLY, A FEW of my own very personal words.

Whatever attitudes I have as a moderator/interviewer did not come from the crib. I learned them the same way I learned to throw a baseball as a kid and change a diaper as a father: I learned the old-fashioned way—by doing.

At the University of Missouri School of Journalism in the 1950s, I learned that the major missions of journalism are to collect, report, and explain.

I took no classes in judging answers and people, column writing, commentating, being a pundit, or expressing opinions. I honed an even-handed approach to interviewing and reporting through ten years as a daily newspaper reporter/editor and ever since in my practice of journalism on public television.

Thus, "fair and balanced" is not a slogan to me. It's a professional way of life.

I have been forever blessed by the fact that Robert MacNeil, my great friend who really invented our program, *The News-Hour*, felt the same way. His early education and discipline came from working on the desk at the Reuters wire service in London and, later, at NBC News and the BBC here and overseas.

Neither MacNeil nor I, as individuals or together as a team, ever saw asking civilized questions, listening politely to the answers, and treating public figures and ideas with courtesy and respect as anything other than simply doing our jobs—being professional.

There was no magic, no heroism, no saintliness involved.

I know that there are folks out there still waiting for me to do something along the lines of the South Carolina congressman's shouting "You lie!" to President Obama. In my case, it would be in response to an answer during a presidential or vice presidential debate—or some other kind of public event on television or elsewhere.

They wait in vain.

One prominent cable talk personality once attacked me on the air for not being aggressive enough during a presidential debate, spitting, "Lehrer's not a *real* journalist!"

To borrow the phrasing of Bill Clinton, I guess it depends on what you mean by "journalist." And by "aggressive."

Debates have qualities that require journalistic skills, tone, and approach, but a journalist participates as a facilitator, not as a gatherer of information. The moderator, journalist or not, must also keep the event fair and moving while staying out of the way.

I think it is safe and proper to note that all reporters—print *or* electronic—are not automatically suited to be moderators. Asking questions to get information for a story can be quite different from asking them to help voters understand what a candidate believes and stands for—and why.

I believe strongly that anyone asked to contribute his or her skills to an exercise as important to the country as a presidential or vice presidential debate has a duty to do so or have a very good reason for not doing so.

To me, it's on a par with pro bono legal or medical work. The only exemption would be for someone whose ego does not permit moving past the idea that a debate is about the moderator. That person should—must!—decline on his/her own to participate.

The rise of new technology and the decline, within some elements, of journalism standards have resulted in a lot of loose-mouthed opinionating on television, blogs, and elsewhere by people who haven't done their homework, don't care about the facts, and disdain balance and fairness—and good taste.

I have no serious problem with any of that. The more voices and views, the better. Always, the better. I do not want anybody shut up. The addition of new and varied and multiple voices in the public mix is terrific for our democracy. I am, in fact, a purist on the First Amendment guarantees of everyone's right to speak, no matter how disagreeable or ridiculous the words may be.

But.

The First Amendment is about a right, not a requirement. It says nothing about *requiring* people to attack or inflame others to get ratings or to be noticed, or to take positions only for votes or to insult people for entertainment value. Or to do whatever any given moderator or questioner/candidate or officeholder may feel compelled by beliefs or ambition to do.

In the new media environment in which presidential elections are conducted now, there is no shortage of opinions—including those of the questioners, in some cases and venues.

I urge everyone involved not to let these opinions slip into the presidential debates.

The only opinions that matter are those of the candidates. Nobody cares what the person asking the questions thinks about anything.

Formats matter but not nearly as much as the conduct of the moderator does, most particularly in any type of the *sole* moderator format. This goes not only for presidential contests but for moderators and participants in all kinds of public debates.

There are readily available examples for how to exchange ideas, disagree, and discuss those disagreements with grace, intelligence, and respect.

The gold standard model is "Shields and Brooks," the Friday night analysis of Mark Shields and David Brooks on our *PBS NewsHour*. Shields is a syndicated columnist; Brooks is a *New York Times* columnist.

There is nothing quite like them and what they do on television.

I was involved in the beginning more than twenty years ago, and I have been a happy moderator of their weekly twelve minutes of quiet analysis ever since.

Shields was one-half of the original duo of "Gergen and Shields" that premiered in 1988. His first teammate was David Gergen, then of *U.S. News & World Report*. The segment became "Shields and Gigot" when Paul Gigot, *The Wall Street Journal*'s Washington columnist, replaced David Gergen in

1993. Gergen had joined the staff of President Bill Clinton, his fifth presidential boss, the first four having been Republicans. Gigot left our Friday night Washington table in 2001 when he moved to New York to become editor of the *Journal*'s editorial page.

David Brooks, then of *The Weekly Standard* and other publications, replaced Gigot, and it's been "Shields and Brooks" from then on.

Mark Shields is a liberal with Democratic political staff ties that go back to William Proxmire, Robert Kennedy, Edmund Muskie, and Morris Udall, among others.

David Brooks is a conservative who came up the journalism/commentary ranks with William F. Buckley Jr.'s *National Review*, *The Wall Street Journal*, and *The Washington Times*, among others.

On *PBS NewsHour*, neither Shields nor Brooks has ever taken a cheap shot against the other.

They do not talk over each other. Or get personal. They do not shout. Or insult. They laugh and smile with each other—like real people. And listen to each other. They report and do their homework. They respect each other's opinions and are both secure enough occasionally even to agree with the other. They also can and do discuss ideas.

Here is a sampling from a January 2010 Shields and Brooks exchange about the new words of "populism" coming from Barack Obama.

BROOKS: He went to Harvard Law School. He went to Columbia University. He appointed Tim Geithner,

Larry Summers. You know, that's not who he is. He is a member of the establishment. He talks like it. He thinks like that.

I happen to have great respect for his analytical abilities and all that. That's who he is. Don't fake it. The lesson of Mitt Romney, don't fake it. Be who you are. And it's just not going to work to fake it.

SHIELDS: I—first of all, all great revolutions are led by aristocrats. That is the reality of history. So, the idea that he went to Harvard Law School does not in any way preclude his leading a populist revolution. Populist has taken on a word among several of my colleagues in the press, not—at least one of whom is here, that it's faintly disrespectful. It's disrespectful. . . .

BROOKS: Listen, populism and elitism are the same thing. They are class prejudices, crude class prejudices that so-and-so, because they are uneducated, is less worthy, or so-and-so, because they are richer or more educated, is unworthy.

They are both crude, crass class prejudices which people can play into or not play into. Redistributing money down is not necessarily populist. But saying all bankers are evil is populist. And, so, it's the crude class prejudice that I think that people are now beginning to play into.

And the only people, by the way, who play into it are phonies. People who are genuinely coming from the working class or representing or feel in their bones working-class values generally don't play those games. Their attitudes are much more complicated and much more real than the fake, "Oh, all those Wall Street types." That is just too generalized.

SHIELDS: I disagree with David's counterfeit distinctions here. I mean, remember that this—this establishmentarian, this president of the [*Harvard Law Review*], what did he do? He became a community organizer. I mean, that's what he did. He turned down Supreme Court clerkships. I mean, he really did go back and try and make a difference. There is that in him.

I would just like to see—Robert Frost once said about Jack—to Jack Kennedy, be more Boston and less Harvard. And Barack Obama is equally as complex and complicated as anybody else.

And I would like to see him be more Chicago and less establishmentarian.

Mark Shields and David Brooks are gentlemen and scholars of civility and discourse. I salute them both for what they do and the way they do it.

That is because I believe as a moderator and as a citizen in the *virtue* of civil discourse as strongly as I believe in the *right* to uncivil discourse.

To repeat the Chautauqua words of Jupiter, Thomas Jefferson's manservant:

"There is nothing more that I can give you today, sir, than I have given you, and that is the truth."

Thank you and good night.

Acknowledgments

Many people helped me. Most are mentioned in the book, so I will not rattle off their names again. I will just thank them all for what they have done to make possible what I do. Debates are collaborative enterprises similar to those of combat and team athletics. Nobody fights, competes—or debates—alone.

I would like to pay a special tribute to two fellow debate panelists. John Mashek was a personal friend who died in 2009. We began our reporting careers together at adjoining desks in the city room of *The Dallas Morning News* in 1959. Peter Jennings, also a friend, lost a fight with cancer in 2005.

There's appreciation due *NewsHour* colleagues Dan Werner and Jim Trengrove. Dan was the producer of the National Issues Convention in Austin, among other breakthrough events of televised civil discourse. Jim produced the *Debating Our Destiny* documentaries, which won many awards. I owe Dan and Jim, as well as Robert MacNeil and all others in the *NewsHour* world, much gratitude for the creative force and grease they have provided me. The same goes for friend Colin Campbell, the head man at Colonial Williamsburg.

Acknowledgments

Annette Miller assisted in the research for this book. So did the solid information from three earlier debate chronicles: *Televised Presidential Debates and Public Policy* by Sidney Kraus, *Presidential Debates: Forty Years of High-Risk TV* by Alan Schroeder, and *Inside the Presidential Debates: Their Improbable Past and Promising Future* by Newton N. Minow and Craig L. Lamay.

Bob Loomis, my editor at Random House, remains the best there is. *Tension City* would have been an unreadable mess without him.

It wouldn't have been even that if it were not for Kate and our three daughters, Jamie, Lucy, and Amanda, to whom the book and everything else in my life that really matters are dedicated.

Index

This is JIM LEHRER's first nonfiction book in more than two decades. He has also written twenty novels, two memoirs, and three plays and is the executive editor of the *PBS NewsHour*. He lives in Washington, D.C., with his novelist wife, Kate. They have three daughters.

ABOUT THE TYPE

This book was set in Sabon, a typeface designed by the well-known German typographer Jan Tschichold (1902–74). Sabon's design is based upon the original letter forms of Claude Garamond and was created specifically to be used for three sources: foundry type for hand composition, Linotype, and Monotype. Tschichold named his typeface for the famous Frankfurt typefounder Jacques Sabon, who died in 1580.